CONNECTED TECHNOLOGY

HOW TO TRANSFORM YOUR BUSINESS WITH CLOUD ACCOUNTING

AMANDA FISHER

Connected Technology
First published in Australia in 2013
www.amandafisher.com.au

Copyright Amanda Fisher 2013

National Library of Australia Cataloguing-in-Publications entry

Author:	Fisher, Amanda
Title:	Connected Technology
ISBN:	9780987486707
Subjects:	Business technology
	Accounting systems
Dewey Number:	658

Disclaimer

All the information, ideas and examples contained within this publication are of the nature of general comments only, and not in any way recommended as individual advice. The intent is to offer a variety of information based on the current state of commercial and industry practice to provide a wider range of choices now and in the future, recognizing that we all have widely diverse circumstances. Should any reader choose to make use of information contained herein without obtaining specific advice for their circumstances, this is their decision, and the contributors, author and publishers do not assume any responsibilities whatsoever under any conditions or circumstances. It is recommended that the reader obtain their own independent advice.

"In life, change is inevitable.
In business, change is vital"

Warren Bennis, founder and chair,
Leadership Institute, University of Southern California

Acknowledgements

As with all endeavours, there are many people who have helped at some point along the way. In fact, too many to acknowledge them all. However, there are some who must be thanked.

Thank you to:

Henry Chin, my very first boss from Norton & Faviell, for teaching me all about debits and credits and basic accounting principles.

Paul Dunn from Buy1Give1 who taught me about marketing and how to run a better accounting business many years ago, who continues to be an inspiration and mentor.

Dale Beaumont from Business Blueprint for giving so freely of his information and widening my knowledge in sales and marketing and cutting edge technology.

Salim Omar for his marketing and sales advice specifically for accountants which has made my business what it is today and led me to writing this book.

Daniel Priestley and Glen Carlson the founders of the KPI program for their insight and assistance in helping me make sense of my life and to define my true purpose.

Andrew Griffiths, thank you for showing me the ropes of writing a book. Without you, the book would have never been started, let alone finished.

My business clients who have allowed me to be a part of their lives – I am honoured and humbled And to those clients who trusted me when I advised them to use Xero Cloud Accounting Systems and who are now enjoying all of the advantages of this brilliant system.

Beryl Lu, Sylvia Cilia, Wendy Thompson, Maryann Neilsen, Susan Raber and Harriet Narwal at Connected Accountants for working like Trojans through our tax season allowing me to take the time to write this book during our busiest part of the year.

Beryl Lu, for believing in me and sticking with me through thick and thin, the good times and the bad – thank you for your loyalty and support.

Meena Berry, my BDM at Xero, for your input and ideas and your unwavering support.

Ronnie Kagan, Sharon Billingham, Shanti Stevens, John Broadbent, Danielle Chiel, Doyle Buehler and Cimone-Louise Fung, and the rest of the KPI SG1 team, thank you for your support and encouragement.

David Masters, Lawrence Crane and Bob Evett for being my friends and colleagues over the years, for mentoring me, for listening and encouraging me, and for believing in me.

For the hard learnt lessons along the way which have made me stronger, wiser and the entrepreneur that I am today.

To the team at Xero – thank you for writing beautiful accounting software. It is a joy to use and has given me a solid basis to work from for the rest of my accounting life.

Stacey Dobis for a fantastic job editing my draft manuscript into a form fit for printing and Julie Renouf and the OpenBook Creative team for putting it all together and arranging for the publishing. A special thanks to Marley Berger who worked over the Easter weekend on the layout to meet my deadlines.

Mum and Dad who expected me to always be the best of the best.

Jean Holland, my best friend, for your never ending positive attitude and get up and go – you continually inspire me to do more.

Last, but definitely not least, my husband, Alf for being my solid rock of support and putting up with my entrepreneurial spirit which takes me off on different tangents and makes our life the rollercoaster ride that it is.

Contents

Foreword

In 1992, Accountants around the world were flocking to a program I'd created known as the Accountants' Boot Camp. By 2000, 17,700 of them had been through the program. (Amanda was one of them, by the way.)

Universally, they told us that the program had 'changed their lives' as we took them from being 'Reporters on History' to 'Creators of History for their Selected Clients'.

And in 1994, I issued an 'edict' to the team, "no one can be allowed to come to the program unless they have an email address." True. Believe it or not, less than 1 in 3 people had email accounts at that time.

The reason for the edict was simple — we had to change the way we were communicating and connecting. We were entering the age of what the Google MD in my home city of Singapore now calls,

'The age of the acceleration of everything.'

In the first few months of 2013, my favourite marketing blogger, Seth Godin, tells us that 'this is now the age of connection.'

And that's why Amanda's superbly written and down-to-earthbook is so timely.

Like my 'you have to have email' edict in 1994, the time will come when you're simply not 'switched on' unless you're accounting in the cloud. And Amanda's book gives you a superb road map to follow to make the transition — well, not just to make it but to make it seamlessly and without pain, fear or loss.

In fact, this book is about the antonyms of those three words — it's about health (your financial health), joy and gain.

Amanda takes you on a great journey here. You'll love her insights, you'll benefit from her wisdom and experience (and the '17 questions you must ask'!) and, above all, you'll connect. As in life, real connection is where the magic starts. And that magic awaits you here.

Paul Dunn
Co-Founder and Chairman - B1G1®

Introduction

Technology over the years has changed the way businesses operate. In today's world there is instant access to information and the expectation of instant responses to all forms of communication; therefore, there has never been a better time to embrace the changes. In fact, if you don't embrace change now, your business may not survive in the future.

We have come a long way in the past 60 years. The first report of the use of electronic computers in business was in 1953. 30 years ago the first major spreadsheet software was released, and around the same time MYOB and QuickBooks business accounting software was first released. Can you imagine doing business without these tools?

In the past five or so years, cloud accounting has arrived and is already revolutionising the way bus-inesses operate. You need to understand the impact cloud accounting can have on your business; the time saving, the ease of use, the information available at your fingertips to help you understand the finance of your business allowing you to make better decisions.

I first started using computers in High School in the 1970's when a computer was a mainframe computer at the local University. When I started work, we sent the accounting entries to a data processing bureau, then a few years later PCs arrived and there was a computer room where only the computer operator was allowed access to process the entries. By the mid 1980's we all had a PC on our desk, Lotus 123, the first spreadsheet software was released, and Attaché, MYOB and QuickBooks and other desktop accounting software was available. Over the past 20 years desktop software has been used by most businesses.

In the past few years, cloud accounting systems have been infiltrating the small business world. They are now firmly established as the way of the future for any business who wants to succeed.

I have seen first-hand with my clients, the benefits to be gained from using cloud accounting systems and know that you too will gain the same benefits if you switch across as well.

In reading this book you will learn:

• What is all the fuss about keeping accounting records and why does it matter how they are kept?

• The difference between desktop software and cloud systems for accounting and bookkeeping.

• The benefits of using cloud accounting systems and how it will improve business operations.

• What options are available and how to determine what is the right one for you.

• How you can use the information available to understand your business figures better.

You will read real cases of clients who have used cloud systems, from new start ups who are using the technology from the beginning, to those who have been using the desktop systems for many years and who have switched. You will find out the reasons behind why they have switched and how the cloud accounting systems have improved their results.

Summary

1   Accounting systems have changed considerably over the past thirty years.

2   The information you are able to gain from a good accounting system today is vastly greater than it was even just five years ago.

3   If you want to stay at the forefront of your field you need to embrace change and that means changing your accounting systems.

4   If you want to stand out from your competitors you need to change the way you do business and the way you view your accounting records and reports.

5   Good accounting systems will provide you with excellent information which will allow you to make better decisions and have more control over your business.

Chapter 1

From mainframe computing to cloud accounting

I am a Chartered Accountant in Australia with over 30 years experience and I have seen massive changes since I first came across the word 'computer' in high school.

High school computer club using university mainframe computer

I went to High School in Halifax, Canada and enjoyed maths and science subjects the most. There weren't any calculators or computers. Any handouts we were given were copies produced from a massive Roneo machine – the forerunner of photocopiers. The school had a Computer Club. There were probably less than 20 of us in the club and I recall being the only girl in the group! We were allowed special access to the Dalhousie University mainframe computer. This meant that on a Saturday morning we would go to the computer section. We would firstly draft out a program in Cobalt (an old computer language). We would then type up the information onto data cards – one line per data card. The card would have holes punched in it based on what we had typed in. We would then put the stack of cards together and hand them into an operator who would put them in the computer for processing. An hour or so later we would get a printout from a dot matrix printer with the results of our work. We would complete serious work e.g. arithmetic calculations and we would do fun stuff like making the printout look like Mickey Mouse. One mistake in a card and you got the wrong result and had to start all over again.

This was a painstaking process and a good lesson on planning ahead so as to minimise the mistakes and to get the right result the first time. Something which isn't very necessary today as it is so much easier to correct mistakes.

First accounting job using ticker tape and processing bureau - 3 day turnaround

My first real job as a trainee accountant was in 1978. There weren't any PC's in those days and a lot of the accounting work was done manually. However, we did use a data processing bureau for some of the work. This system required that we work out what accounting entries we needed processed, one of the staff would type this into a machine that would produce a ticker tape and this would be sent off to the data processing bureau once a day. The resulting report would be returned usually three or four days later. If you made one mistake or missed one entry, you then had to go through the whole process again.

With deadlines for getting work completed for our clients, it became imperative that we got the entries correct the first time, as every time we got it wrong, the work would be delayed by three days. When we were happy with the figures, the secretaries would then type up the financial statements and tax returns using typewriters.

Second accounting job with personal computers and dedicated data entry operator

A couple of years later, I changed jobs at a time when PCs had started to be used more often. However, in this case there were only a few computers for an office of 30 or so accountants. The computers were in a special room which was climate controlled and only the computer operators were allowed in. In this system, we wrote out the entries and gave them to the computer operator who would do the data entry and provide the printed reports for our review. The time had reduced significantly to get the results, although subject to the amount of work piled up, it could still take a day or two to get the reports back.

The financial statements and tax returns were still being prepared using typewriters by the ladies in the 'typing pool'.

Third accounting job with PC's in computer room and staff with access to process data

My next job was a couple of years later and there was still a computer room with PCs, but now the accounting staff were allowed to process the entries themselves. There were more PCs and as soon as the staff member had processed the entries, the reports were immediately available.

PC's on everyone's desk and first release of Lotus 123 spreadsheet software - 5 year projections

Then in the mid 1980's a massive revolution occurred when we all got PCs on our desk. Now we had the ability to instantly process work and obtain the results ourselves. In 1983 the first killer program for PCs was released – Lotus 123 spreadsheet software. I recall the day this was loaded onto the computers and my boss at the time challenged me to produce a five-year projection of tax payable for a large client group allowing for three or four different alternatives as to how the income was distributed each year. I was given less than a week to complete the task and it was to be done in my own time. That meant that I had to learn how to use Lotus 123 and then set up the spreadsheets to do the calculations. It was fantastic, the spreadsheets made the calculations so much easier and it was so simple to change one factor and it immediately updated all the other figures. This was the WOW of this time period for anyone working with numbers.

MYOB for business clients

In the early 1980's accounting software was released for general usage – Attaché, MYOB, QuickBooks and many others. As accountants we provided advice to our business clients on how to change their systems to use the best software available and I was instrumental in installing and establishing accounting systems using Attaché to a number of our major business clients. These installations took many days to undertake and usually a couple of weeks of solid work just to get it set up.

Then there was ongoing time spent to make sure it was working properly and the figures produced made sense and were accurate. The clients' staff had to be trained on how to use the software and thus the installation of these types of accounting systems was both costly in money terms and also in the time involved. Over the next few years MYOB became the desktop software of choice for most small to medium sized businesses. This new software meant that everyone who was intending to use it needed to be trained. MYOB training courses were fully booked and over the years MYOB continues to be taught in TAFE, evening and community colleges and by private training organisations.

These desktop software packages were another giant leap forward in the accounting process for business owners and their bookkeepers to save significant time. The old requirement of hand-writing up a cashbook was no longer required, although a lot of businesses continued to do so for many years. Like anything new, there is fear of change generally and for some, there was concern about whether the information would be correct and whether it was safe. They also found it easier to look up entries in the cashbook because they were more familiar with it.

From the mid 1980's for almost 20 years there was no real alternative. The desktop software was upgraded over the years and was better than when it was first released, but fundamentally the systems were the same as they were 20 years ago.

Cloud accounting systems

The latest revolution started less than 10 years ago when a number of savvy entrepreneurs saw the benefit the internet could provide to create a different type of accounting system. The internet would allow business systems to be more integrated, efficient, and easily accessible. Welcome to Cloud Accounting. This accounting framework allows for the use of an accounting system via the internet; thereby creating a collaboration of many different users to process accounting data simultaneously.

There are many providers of Cloud Accounting Systems and more are created every day. The one thing they all have in common is the use of cutting edge technology to provide solutions. Some are easy to use, some are free, some integrate with other systems, and some have arrangements with the banks to allow bank statement information to be fed into the accounting system automatically. But they all allow for access by different people in different locations at the same time looking at the same information.

Summary

1   It is important to watch out for changes going on around you.

2   It is imperative to embrace those changes or be left behind.

3   Taking risks with new innovations and technology will give you the jump start on your competitors and will make you stand out from the crowd.

4   Consider the benefits of the decisions you make for the long-term even though they may cost time and money in the short-term.

Chapter 2

Why keep accounting records?

The multiple hats of a business owner

Legal requirements to help determine income for tax purposes

Your first hat as a business owner is to contribute your fair share of taxes to the community.

But why do you have to keep accounting records? You didn't go into business to be an accountant or a bookkeeper, but yet this must be done. Accounting records are required to be kept to allow you to report your earnings so that you can pay the correct amount of tax.

In the 13th century business owners in Italy required written records of business dealings in order to ensure their managers were honest. These developed into the current double entry system that we know today - the basis for computer accounting systems.

With the Industrial Revolution, governments increased taxation requirements and the need for accurate accounting records became imperative to ensure taxes were paid correctly.

Today, most countries require business owners to report their annual income figures to the government and to pay tax on these amounts. In addition, there are Sales Taxes, Goods and Services Taxes, Value Added Taxes and other transaction taxes depending upon where you operate your business. All of these are required to be reported to the tax man on a regular basis.

Legal requirements for reporting to shareholders of the business

Your second hat is that of the owner of the business.

Although you may own and run your own business, there is still a requirement that the financial figures of the business be reported to the owners of the business. This may seem strange when you are in business for yourself and you own the business.

However, you need to look at your business from different angles. One of those angles is from that of the owner or shareholder of the business. This person wants the business to be showing good profits, to have a strong balance sheet and to have sufficient working capital to continue to operate into the future.

Business owners who review their trading results and financial reports regularly are more successful than those who don't. From my experience, business owners who abdicate responsibility for the accounting and don't want to see their figures, go out of business. The reason for this is that they have no idea of whether they are actually making a profit or not. Just watching how much money you have in the bank does not necessarily mean you are making money.

Abdicating responsibility

Unfortunately there are some people who really should not be in business for themselves. These are the ones who abdicate all responsibility for the parts of the business they don't enjoy or for which they have no aptitude. To be successful in any business you need to have a working knowledge of all facets of the business. That includes sales and marketing, finance, employment requirements, and the everyday running of the business. Larger businesses will have staff who specialise in different areas and they may not have any understanding of the other areas. When you start out in business, you don't have that luxury and you must be the wearer of multiple hats.

Cathy ran a business for a couple of years. It wasn't really making any money. She didn't like managing staff, she wasn't good at numbers and her forte was supposed to be in sales and marketing. She put a manager in charge of the business and told him to run it and manage the staff, she appointed someone else with no expertise in the area to look after paying the staff, she only turned up at the business premises two days a week (the business was open six days a week) and she didn't want to know about anything except what she was doing – the sales and marketing and unfortunately she wasn't very smart at that.

After a disastrous marketing campaign, the business folded. She didn't understand the figures and didn't want to know anything about them. If she had done so, she probably wouldn't have undertaken the marketing campaign the way she did, as it was never going to make the business money. The campaign consisted of a discounted price for a package of services that was actually below cost. Initially she thought she was doing well as 1000 customers bought the package, she used the money to buy some equipment which was needed to provide the services and then for about four months her business was busy providing the services to the 1000 customers.

However, whilst this was going on, the rest of the business offerings were ignored and regular customers became disenfranchised and went elsewhere. As the money began to run out and there were still services to provide to these new customers, Cathy finally realised that something was wrong, but blamed it all on the business manager and the staff. In fact, the problem started with the pricing of the offering which was just far too low to be sustainable.

The finances of every business are vital to ensure that your business flourishes. Decisions about every facet of the business need to be made after careful consideration of how they will impact the future.

Accounting reports for credit applications with suppliers

Your third hat is that of a purchaser of goods and services from others.

When you ask your suppliers to provide you with goods and services you have two options. One is to pay cash up-front at the time of the purchase. The other is to ask your suppliers to extend credit to you that will allow you to pay your account some time after the date of purchase. This commonly is seven or 30 days. Suppliers want to know whether you are good for the money if they sell you their goods and services without payment at the time. Most suppliers will want to see a copy of your financial statements before they extend credit. These people will be looking at whether you have a business which is profitable, how much working capital is in the business and how much you owe to other people. Some will limit the amount of credit extended to you based on their review of your financial statements.

Accounting reports for finance applications

Your fourth hat is similar to the third, but this is where you are seeking a loan or finance from a bank or other financial institution.

Banks and financial institutions want even more information than suppliers to provide you with credit. Typically they will require financial statements from the past two years at least and projected income for the following year, details of who you are and your business experience, what other assets you may own and a myriad of other questions.

The fundamental figures they are looking at to start with though are the financial statements. This is the first part of an application that they will look at and if your financial results are not good, they will not often take your application any further.

Accounting reports for potential investors in the business

Your fifth hat is when you are seeking investors or partners to join you in the business.

For some of you, you may never wear this hat. However, for those who want to expand the business and grow beyond a certain size, this may be your only option to achieve those goals.

A potential investor in a business wants to know all about you, your background, what you know about the business you are running, how many years have you been in business, how profitable the business is, what assets are in the business, what intellectual property you may have which may not be shown in the financial statements and overall what do your financial statements show.

In these situations, your financial statements are important and your projections of cash flow and profit for the future are critical. The projections are determined using your current financial statements as a base.

Business operations reporting for decision making

The sixth and most important hat is that of the business owner and decision maker.

Can you imagine going on holiday not knowing where you are going to go or how to get there? Now occasionally some of us do this for our holiday, just light out and decide where we go each day without any plan. However, I am sure that you wouldn't go on holiday without having decided where you are going to go and how you plan to get there.

You need to run your business the same way. You have to determine where you want to go and then from there you can determine how you will get there. In order to assist in this process, though, you need to understand where you are starting from. This can be determined from your financial statements. These show you how much income you have, what your expenses are and what profit you have made. They also show how much money your customers or clients owe you, how much you owe to your suppliers and any loans you owe to the bank or other financial institution. When you have these figures readily available it is much easier to make decisions about what you need to do to get to where you want to go.

You may need to decide whether to employ another sales person, whether to buy a piece of equipment, whether to buy your business premises, whether to spend more on advertising, whether to increase your selling prices, whether you need to negotiate a better price for your purchases and a myriad of other decisions that need to be made on a daily basis. Without accurate, up-to-date financial statements you will not be able to make the best decisions.

Summary

1   As a business owner you need to have information available for a multitude of different purposes.

2   Without good information, you do not have the ability to make an informed decision about your business.

3   Different people associated with your business will want different information, so you need to have the right accounting system so that the information is available quickly and easily at any time.

4   Planning your business, setting goals and checking on your progress are vital to any successful business owner.

Chapter 3

Problems with current desktop software

Desktop accounting software has done a wonderful job for the past 30 years since the early versions of the software were first released. However, the world has changed significantly during this time with the advent of widely used internet, Google, Social Media and a myriad of other applications. We now all expect everything to be done instantly including our accounting and bookkeeping processes.

The old desktop software simply cannot keep up with the new requirements.

Requirements to manually back-up regularly

When using desktop software you have to regularly perform back-ups to ensure data is not lost. These back-ups should be completed daily or once a week at a minimum; however, you may be like the majority of business owners who fail to back-up regularly at all. You may rely on the copies you send into your accountant on a quarterly basis as being your back-up or you may remember to back-up occasionally to an external drive or USB.

If you forget to or simply don't back-up and your computer fails, you have lost all the data entry you have done since the last time you performed a back-up. If you were living in Brisbane in early 2011 or New York/New Jersey in 2012 and relied on your computer which became waterlogged with the flooding, then anything which was on your computer would have been lost. If the back-up copies were also in the same location, you may have lost those too.

Alternatively, you may simply have a computer where the hard-drive just simply stops working. You may be able to recover some of the data, if you are lucky. You will usually have to re-enter some of the information and depending on your business re-constructing the figures can be an extremely difficult task.

Loss of Data

John runs a small business providing professional services to other businesses. He has a bookkeeper who comes in once a month to do some of his bookkeeping and to check the figures, but most of the data entry he does himself. His desktop accounting software is on his laptop. He does back-up regularly – usually once a week or so.

One day the computer just stopped working. John took it to his IT expert and asked him to fix it. When the IT man opened up the laptop, he found that the hard-drive had literally burned. It was black. This is unusual, as often the problem is just that the mechanism stops working in which case an IT expert is able to recover the majority of the data. In this case though – everything was lost...gulp.

There was nothing that could be done to retrieve any of the information. The back-up of the computer had been done about a week to 10 days previously, and so John had to painstakingly re-construct his accounting records for that period and all his other records, document files, correspondence and so on. John rang my office as soon as he found out and asked that we set up a cloud accounting system for him immediately so that he won't have to worry about this happening again in the future.

Requirements to back-up data to send to your accountant

With desktop software literally being on the desktop of a particular computer, every time you want to get advice from your accountant, or you need to get the accountant to prepare some figures for the tax man, you need to do a back-up of the data file and send it to your accountant.

Up until a few years ago, the main way to send data to your accountant was via email (if the file was small enough). If the file was larger you would either put it on a disc or USB drive and post it or drop it into your accountant. The time required for this process was in some cases significant; particularly if you chose to either spend money on a courier, or spend your own time to hand deliver it to your accountant.

When your accountant received the file, they had to open the back-up copy and load it onto their computer system. This could take up to 15 or 20 minutes depending upon the size of the file and the system your accountant used to ensure all the staff in their office could access the file. This would have been an extra cost to you as most accountants charge you for loading your records onto their system.

Accountants only see figures when file is sent to them

The biggest downside to desktop accounting software is that your accountant only sees your financial figures either when you send the back-up file to them or when they come to your business to check them out.

For some, this means your accountant only sees your figures once every three months. For others, this will be only once a year, often many months after the end of the financial year. Thus your accountant cannot provide any advice about your business or let you know if your business is not doing as well as expected in sufficient time to allow you to make decisions to improve the situation.

When your accountant only sees the figures after the end of the year, they have no idea of how well or not your business has been trading. It may be too late for any changes to be made to the way you do business and your business may even be insolvent without you being aware of it. A business is insolvent when you are not able to pay your suppliers, repayments on loans, taxes and so on by the date they are due.

The worst part of your business becoming insolvent is it may have been prevented if your accountant had seen the figures earlier they may have been able to provide advice which could have improved the results.

Upfront purchase price and ongoing support fees

Desktop software is sold with an upfront purchase price which usually provides you with 12 months of support and updates. The updates may be improvements to the software or simply changes in tax rates from one year to the next. When you start out in business, most people don't usually have large cash resources to commence with and the requirement to pay money upfront to purchase accounting software adds a burden to a start-up business. In addition, you may also need to take some training courses to learn how to use the software.

Need to load software onto computer

Some business owners are tech savvy, but if you are not, then when you buy desktop software you may need to find a local IT expert to come to your business to load up the software and make sure that it works with your printers. The IT expert may need to set up a local area network so that your staff are able to access the accounting software from different computers in your business. This adds to the cost of the upfront purchase.

On one computer - therefore have to be on site for data entry and to review reports

Originally, desktop software was designed to be on one computer, which meant any of your staff who needed access to the financial records of the business would have to use the same computer for it. Over time, it has been possible for IT people to network the computers in a business so different staff members in the same office have access to the software. This does not always work well as the speed of use of the software can be slow with multiple users and sometimes there are issues if two people try and access the same part of the software at exactly the same time.

All reporting must be done from the computer at your business premises and unless you plan ahead and print out reports to take to a meeting or to review at home at the end of the day, you would not be able to access them.

The accessibility of the data has been increased in recent years with the ability to access other computers via remote login software. These can work well, although speed of use of the software may be slow and there may be security issues with the connection between the locations. The biggest downside to most of these systems is the person who is logging in remotely cannot print out any reports; they can only view them on their computer screen.

No integration with bank accounts

Desktop systems are self contained. Meaning they don't allow for integration with anything else. Bank statement information has to be manually entered into the software. There is no ability to import this data into the software to reduce the data entry time.

After entering in the details of each bank transaction, you or your bookkeeper then have to manually reconcile the bank account details in the software with the details shown on your bank statement issued by the bank. This can be a long and laborious task, particularly if your business has a large number of transactions. You may, in fact, need to have the bank account reconciled on a daily basis if you have a high volume of transactions which is time consuming work and costly.

No dashboard reporting

But what is dashboard reporting? Think of the dashboard in your car. It shows you how fast you are going, how many revs you are using, the temperature of the car, how much fuel you have in the tank, how far you have travelled, whether you have your lights on and a number of other useful pieces of information to assist you whilst you are driving. Well a dashboard in accounting terms is similar; it tells you your current position, it provides information about where you are going, it highlights key figures and provides other useful data about your business.

Dashboard reporting is a one page summary report or an on screen display which shows all of the key figures for your business in the one location. A dashboard report may show you the balance in your bank account, the amount owing to you by your customers or clients, the amount you owe to your suppliers. It may also show how much revenue you have made for the month and year to date, or the amount owing to the tax man.

It is a snapshot of your business at a point in time. Every day the dashboard numbers will be different. Unfortunately, due to the nature of desktop software, these reports are simply not available.

Limited reporting capabilities - eg. no graphs

Desktop software was originally written at a time when financial reports were used purely for reporting to the tax man and were not used to provide information to business owners to help them run their business. The reports were designed to simply be a listing of figures. This is fine if you actually really understand the figures, but if not, too bad. There are no graphs produced from the desktop software systems which can provide a visual analysis of the figures.

Most business owners don't look at the reports

The reality is that you probably don't look at the reports from your desktop software very often. Even when you do, the information will be historical and potentially out of date by the time the report is issued. If you wait for the bank statement to be issued by your bank and to arrive in the mail after the end of the month, you will be lucky if your financial reports for the month are ready within two weeks. This means that you are looking at some figures which are from six weeks earlier.

If your business had a very profitable first three weeks of the month, but did not trade well in the fourth week and the first two weeks of the next month; the reports will not give you an accurate picture of the trading results. It won't be until two weeks after the end of the next month that you will start to see what is happening, some seven weeks later. You will not be able to make good decisions using these types of reports and you will probably make decisions based on your gut instincts rather than based on the evidence of what is actually happening in your business.

Summary

1   Desktop accounting software has many disadvantages in today's world of internet connectivity.

2   You cannot share your financial information easily with others.

3   The data is kept on one computer.

4   There are no easy to read dashboard reports which summarise on one page the status of your business.

5   You have to remember to manually back-up your data regularly.

6   In the event of a disaster in your business premises of any kind, you may lose all your data or some of it.

7   Your accountant will only see your trading results when you send the figures to them.

8   All the transactions have to be entered manually, there is no automation.

Chapter 4

Benefits of cloud accounting systems

Available anytime, anywhere with internet access

Cloud accounting systems are internet based; therefore you must have an internet connection to use them. However, as long as you do have an internet connection, you are able to access your business data any time of the day, anywhere you may be.

You could be on the beach with a laptop, tablet or mobile phone. Imagine being in an internet café in a third world country, at home, or in a coffee shop on the other side of the world. It doesn't matter where you are; you can access your accounting records anywhere.

Now, I know it isn't everyone's idea of fun to be on holiday and looking up the accounting records of your business. But then again, when was the last time you took a holiday and weren't worried about whether there would be enough money in the bank to cover your financial commitments while you were away and had to phone in regularly to find out how much income had been banked?

Now you can take a holiday and still have access to the information if you want or need to.

Integration with banks to get daily bank data feeds

This is one of the WOW factors when using cloud accounting systems. Most systems are set-up so that overnight your bank will push out the details of all your transactions from the day before directly into your cloud accounting system. The benefits of this are massive. Firstly, this is where you will see time savings. Instead of having to type in every entry from the bank statement, now all the information is already typed into the system for you. Your job now is to identify what the entry is about and either match it to an invoice or decide the best place to allocate it.

For example, if the entry is a deposit into your bank account from a customer, you would need to find the invoice you issued then match it so the cash receipt would be reconciled. If the entry is a payment and you had not entered the bill to pay into the system previously, you would identify what the expense was for (say it was for your telephone account) then you would allocate it to telephone expenses and that entry would be reconciled.

In addition to saving time, this also reduces the opportunity for errors and incorrect allocations of the bank transactions.

Security of data - rack systems and regular back-ups

Security of data is an important issue for all business owners and you need to be conscious of this too. You need to ensure the data you enter into the cloud accounting system is held in a secure location and the security of the website you are using is top notch.

The best cloud accounting systems are using major rack storage systems around the world. These storage systems are rooms and rooms of hard drives stored in racks (hence the name) all connected and kept sterile at constant temperatures. The best systems also require that the data is backed up regularly, preferably every few minutes and the data is also copied onto the rack storage in multiple locations around the world.

When you have your data stored in multiple locations around the world and backed up regularly, the possibility of losing your data is very low and the security is very high.

No upfront cost - regular monthly fee only

Software as a Service (SAAS) is the term used for any software where there are no upfront fees and the costs to use the system are monthly fees only. All cloud accounting software is invoiced as SAAS.

No installation or information technology (IT) expertise required

The benefit of a SAAS system is you don't need to call in the IT experts to set it up for you. You just sign up for the system online and you get immediate access through a login. From there, you are able to invite other users to log into your accounting data. This means you can access the system yourself, and you can have your staff at the business use it, you may have an offsite bookkeeper who can access it and then there is your accountant who must have access to it too.

Dashboard

The dashboard is the name used for the first screen you see when you log into your cloud accounting system. It shows all the key figures for your business in the one location. Most dashboards show you the balance in your bank account, the amount owing to you by your customers or clients, and the amount you owe to your suppliers. It may also show how much revenue you have made for the month and year to date, or the amount owing to the tax man.

Depending upon which cloud accounting system you decide to use, you may have the ability to choose some of the information which is on the dashboard.

The dashboard report is a snapshot of your business at the point in time when you login. Every time a figure is changed, the dashboard will change too.

A quick review of the dashboard is a great way to start the working day. It allows you to make decisions with the knowledge of exactly how your business is running on the day.

Easy customisation of invoice templates

Most cloud accounting systems allow for some flexibility in the layout of your invoices. Some have less flexibility than others. But at the end of the day, the most important parts of your invoice are the name and details of your customer, what they bought, and the amount they owe you so you can get paid. It actually doesn't need to be a work of art. It needs to be easy to identify that the invoice has come from your business, so it is best to have your logo on it and be sure that it shows how your customer or client can pay you.

I have included some examples of invoice styles at *www.connectedtechnologybook.com/resources/invoices.*

Reporting

Cloud accounting systems, like desktop software, have built-in reports, a number of which are standard accounting reports, like the profit and loss statement and balance sheet. Because of the way the systems have been written, you are able to export the data to a number of different programs.

One of the export options is usually the ability to export into a spreadsheet program. When you have your data in a spreadsheet, you are able to manipulate the data to provide a myriad of other reports and graphical representations of your key figures.

The downside of being able to manipulate data in a spreadsheet program is the risk of losing the integrity of the data as it can be quite easy to delete figures or change them. However, used correctly this can provide some very useful reporting options.

In addition, the reports are usually able to be exported into PDF format so they cannot be changed by setting a password locked file. These reports are great for keeping a static record of the information at a particular point in time and are good for back-up copies of your data.

Integration with other business systems

Have you been running your business using multiple systems? For example, you have one for accounting, another for your sales people to keep track of potential customers or clients, another as a database to send out emails, and others specialised for your industry? And let me guess, none of them talk to the others? You have to enter the same information potentially into a number of these different systems; thereby, risking the integrity of the data.

Now you have the possibility to use systems which integrate with one another. You can enter a potential customer into your Customer Relations Management (CRM) system, and when they buy from you, they will automatically be added into your customer list in your accounting system, and into your email database. How good would that be?

This is one of the major benefits of most cloud accounting systems. Some cloud accounting systems are even written in an open language so developers are able to program them to integrate with each other.

The time saving and cost saving from these integrated systems can be significant.

Mobile apps

The bigger cloud accounting systems have recently released mobile apps which are able to be used on iPhones, Android phones, iPads and other mobile devices. These are especially useful for tradesmen and businesses who service the end consumer at their home or business premises. When the job is completed, you can log into your mobile app, enter the details of the invoice and email it directly to the customer whilst on the spot. For business owners, you are able to quickly check your financial position whilst out of the office at any time.

Saving Time with On the Job Invoicing

Bob is a local electrician. He mainly works fixing up problems at people's homes and does some work wiring up offices too. Like most tradesmen, he used to do his work and handwrite an invoice when the job was completed and then in the evening after the end of the day's work, he would enter the information into a spreadsheet. His wife would keep track of who had paid and who hadn't and chase up payments and generally do the rest of the paperwork for the business.

Bob was encouraged to switch to a cloud accounting system which had a mobile app. Now when he finishes the job, he logs into the mobile app on his phone and enters the details of the job. This enables him to be able to immediately email the invoice to the customer. Bob now finds that he has time in the evenings to spend with his kids and is much less stressed about the business finances.

Real time collaboration with advisors

This is the big WOW factor for cloud accounting systems. Not only do you have your accounting system up to date daily, but now your bookkeeper and your accountant have access to the figures anytime, anywhere as well.

Your accountant is able to check in to your business figures on a regular basis and make sure you are on track. They will be able to see when business is doing well and when it isn't. Your accountant can now keep an eye on some of the obvious key performance indicators which show how the business is doing.

When you have a decision to make, you can call your accountant and talk about what you plan to do while you are both looking at the same financial data onscreen. Gone are the days of printing out reports and having a face to face meeting. Now you may choose to have this type of conversation over the phone.

Summary

1   You can access your accounting information anywhere, any time as long as you have internet access.

2   Your bookkeeper and accountant can also access your accounting information at any time and they don't have to wait for you to send them a copy of your file.

3   Integration with bank data feeds saves data entry time and allows your accounting records to be up to date every day.

4   Integration with other systems means no more multiple databases, no more duplication of information from one system to another. Another time saver.

5   Your data is safe and secure and automatically backed up regularly without you doing anything.

Chapter 5

Obstacles to using cloud based accounting systems

There are probably a number of reasons why you would not want to use cloud accounting systems. Many of you will fear change as you may not under-stand exactly what the system does and how it works.

Need to learn a new system

One of the main reasons you may not want to change is you will need to learn a whole new bookkeeping system. You will also need to learn how to invoice, how to process receipts and payments, how to run your payroll, how to reconcile the bank account, what reports to create and the list goes on.

Yes, there is the need to learn the new system and depending upon which system you choose and how quickly you learn, it may take you anything from a few hours to a few days to get up and running.

Good news though, cloud accounting systems perform exactly the same functions as desktop software, just in a different, usually, much simpler way, making the learning easy.

Just like anything new, you need to get used to it. I recommend spending the time at the beginning to learn how to use the system correctly and how to get the reports you need. Eventually it becomes simple and easy to use.

If you do not take the time to learn the new system, and decide to pick it up as you go, it will seem like a difficult process. You may get frustrated with how long it is taking to get to the point where you are able to use the system without thinking hard about how to do what you want to do.

However, if you are new to business and just starting out, the benefit of spending some time to understand the cloud accounting system, how to use it, and what reporting you can get from it, will give you a head start with controlling your business from day one. Most new start-up owners are not interested in the financial side of the business early on, but taking the time to learn it when first starting the business will help you in the long-run. You will have information available whenever you need it to make informed decisions about the direction of your business.

Using cloud system from start-up with no knowledge of bookkeeping

A couple who were working for two separate employment agencies decided they wanted to set up their own business. They pitched for some contracts in their spare time and won a couple and so the business was created. However, setting up a business is not quite this simple as the two of them have found out over the ensuing months. The decision was that Judy would be the lucky one who would look after the bookkeeping with assistance from the team at my office.

Both Judy and Joe are tech savvy and up with the latest in computer technology. As a result, we recommended that they use a cloud accounting system for their bookkeeping as we knew it would be a logical option for them. We started from the beginning and through one on one training, emails and phone calls; we have trained Judy to the point where she understands the fundamentals of a profit and loss account, and the balance sheet. She knows how to reconcile the bank account, run the payroll, issue invoices and receive money against invoices and so on.

Judy has learnt the basics of bookkeeping in a short period and is functional using the cloud accounting system. As more time goes by, she will learn more and understand the financial aspects of the business better.

Cost of learning new system, downtime whilst converting and learning

Hand in hand with taking the time to learn the system at the beginning is the cost associated with not being productive in your business and the extra time it will take to undertake the basic processes during the learning period. However, I have found that business owners who have switched to cloud accounting systems have saved significant time when they have the system up and running and know how to use it.

A little time spent early on will save you a lot more time in the future. Once you have converted to a cloud accounting system, you will wonder why you put up with the clumsiness of the old desktop software for so long.

For new start-up owners, you will reap the benefit of understanding the bookkeeping function early on in the business and a further benefit of starting with a cloud accounting system is you will start with the most advanced technology currently available to assist you with your business finances.

Conversion of data from old system - loss of history in the one place

If you have a well-established business which has operated for many years using the same desktop accounting software, then you will have a massive volume of historical data in your accounting records. You will be able to report on how much each customer or client has spent with you over the years, you will be able to check expenses over time and be able to report historical information for many years in the past.

The shame about desktop software and the old types of accounting systems is they were written to record historical data. That is, they were designed to record the figures from the past and were not designed to project figures into the future.

The benefit of cloud accounting systems is they have been designed to allow for easy forward projections of cash flow and future profits. They even provide current data to enable future possibilities to be explored.

There are two options if you have a lot of historical information in your desktop accounting software. One option is to take the opportunity to establish the new cloud accounting system with a clean slate and only current customers/clients, suppliers; employees and so on are entered into the new system. If you need to refer back to the history, you simply open the desktop accounting software to check the information there.

The second option is to import some of the historical data into the cloud accounting system. Depending upon which cloud system you use, you may be able to import the data for some years of history. This can be useful to allow for comparison reporting within the cloud system; however, it is time consuming to convert the data and the costs may outweigh any benefits that might be gained.

Lack of trust of internet generally

The internet has been in use now for 20 years and you may consider you do not trust it when it comes to the financial data of your business. The internet first went public in 1989 and through the 1990's it gained popularity and saw astronomical growth. Since then, the internet has continued to grow and become a part of our daily lives throughout the world.

The important question to ask when deciding whether to use cloud accounting systems is whether you are willing to embrace technology and be a business which is keeping up with the changing world, or whether you want to stay with the older systems which will in time become obsolete.

Where is the data? Is it mine or does someone else own it?

It is difficult for most of us to understand how the internet works and where everything is really stored. The internet is simply a name for millions of computers which are connected to each other. There are big data storage facilities throughout the world, known as *rack systems*. This is where the majority of the data is held. Banks use rack systems to store your bank information, and cloud accounting systems use them too. The companies who own the rack systems have high security; they are massive buildings full of millions of hard disks on which all the data is stored.

Your financial data is always yours. There are ways to safeguard your data and you should only use a reputable cloud accounting system. You should consider copying your data off the cloud accounting system from time to time so that you have your own record of the information too.

Concern over security of data from other people accessing it

For most people, this is the biggest concern of all. You don't want anyone else to access your business data, whether it is the banks, the tax man, or an unrelated party.

Cloud accounting systems have been designed to be highly secure with you having control over the people who you want to have access to your data. You control who you invite into your records and you have control over removing their rights to that access.

A number of the cloud accounting systems have arrangements with many banks and financial institutions allowing data from your bank to be transferred into the cloud accounting system. In order for the banks to agree to provide this data, the cloud accounting system has to prove it has sufficient security measures in place so as not to interfere with the integrity of the data or to allow any unauthorised access during the data transmission procedures. These tests require top level security and as such should provide you with comfort about the safety of your data from other people accessing it.

Ability to scale with your growing business

When you are considering a system to use, you need to look at the needs of your business today and think about your plans for the future. What are the possible changes you will be required to make in the future? It will always be a better solution to choose a system allowing you to grow and continue to use the system, rather than start with one which does what you need to start with, but won't allow for expansion and growth into the future.

Most of the cloud accounting systems allow for some scalability into the future. The biggest restriction which is likely to affect your decision to implement a cloud accounting system solution will be the volume of transactions you process. The more transactions; the slower the system is likely to be, particularly when you want to look up specific transactions or when you want to obtain the reports. The more data that is in the database to be checked and reported on, the longer it will take to process.

Speed of internet connection

All cloud accounting systems operate through the internet. A good reliable internet connection is thus a prerequisite to obtaining the benefits of cloud accounting. If your business is located in an area with poor or unreliable internet access, then this will not be an option for you at this time.

Summary

1   Time and cost of learning a new system.

2   Conversion of data from previous system to the new.

3   Lack of trust with the internet generally and specifically concerns over the security of your business data.

4   Concern about your bank accessing your financial records.

Chapter 6

Training and conversion

Learning options – teach yourself, help centres, formal face to face training, training videos/programs

Depending upon which cloud accounting system you choose, there may be various options available to you to learn how to use it properly.

All systems have a Help Centre which will have information on how to use the system and frequently asked questions. Some have extensive information in the Help Centre with screen shots and step-by-step processes; some have short videos show ing you what to do. Most have an option to log a support query if you cannot find the answer to your question within the Help Centre.

In some cases, the users of the system have developed training courses, both formal face-to-face and informal sessions which are an excellent place to start. As more and more information is available online, you will find there will be webinars and videos that will help you too.

One important factor in deciding on a cloud accounting system to use, is to find an accounting firm that uses the system you want to use. They will be able to assist with support questions and may have staff who are able to provide training which will relate specifically to you and your specific business needs. Each business is different, so, although the training courses are a great way to get the basics under your belt, it may be worth spending a couple of hours with an experienced user of the system specifically talking about your business and how to use the system to your best advantage.

Both business owner and bookkeeper need to know how to use the system

It is imperative that you know the basics of using the system and particularly how to get the reports and information you need on a regular basis easily. As the business owner, you do not necessarily need to know exactly how the entire system works, although it is good if you do. Rather as long as you are able to access the information when you need it, you will have the details which will assist you in your decision making.

Most cloud accounting systems have different levels of user access, so you may have one employee who is able to enter the basic information into invoices, but doesn't have the authority to approve the invoices. You may have a different staff member, or bookkeeper, who prepares the payroll and does nothing other than that. You may have someone else again who you want to do the bank reconciliations and pay your bills. Each of these people would need to be properly trained in the part of the system that they are required to use in their day to day work. The beauty of cloud accounting systems is all of these various people are able to access your data file at the same time and do their various jobs without upsetting the work being done by the others.

Knowledge of the system, learnt early on in the installation process, will provide valuable benefits in the future.

Benefits of Training

Steve ran a large manufacturing business which manufactured and installed windows in new large buildings. The business employed 20 or more staff and had a full-time in-house bookkeeper. Recently, Steve decided to set up his own business providing consulting services and manufacturing windows for small jobs. He started as a one man business and over the first 12 months took on some casual workers when he needed help with the manufacturing side of the business.

He decided to use a cloud accounting system so that he could obtain regular advice on the figures. He attended a one day training course on how to use the cloud system and then followed up with a one on one training session for a couple of hours. A few phone call discussions later and he had learnt the basics sufficiently enough to be able to enter his invoices, and reconcile his bank account.

Six months later, the business was doing well, there were a number of jobs booked in and Steve found he simply didn't have the time to do the bookkeeping side of the business. He employed a part-time admin assistant who then was trained on the cloud accounting system and with assistance *from my accounting staff, has taken over the day to day bookkeeping functions from Steve.*

He is able to log into his cloud accounting system to check how the figures are looking without having to do the daily processing. In addition, he has employed a payroll expert to process his payroll on a weekly basis as the wages change every time depending upon who has worked and what hours they worked. The payroll person has never set foot on the business premises and does it all from home.

Conversion of data - how much, how far back

This is the 64 million dollar question. How much data do you transfer into your new cloud accounting system? I referred to this previously and the answer comes down to a cost benefit analysis. You need to ask yourself the following questions. How often would you need to go back to the old data? How long before you won't be accessing the old data? How much benefit would you gain by having reports which have historical data on them to compare the current figures to? How much time and money will it cost to convert the historical data into the cloud accounting system? These answers need to be reviewed and the benefits compared to the cost of conversion of the data from your old desktop system into the cloud accounting system.

The cost of conversion will depend in part at least on what system you are using currently, how easy it is to export the data from the old system and in what format, whether you need to tidy up the old data and delete records/details of customers or clients or suppliers who you no longer deal with.

There is no right or wrong answer to this question, but a good rule of thumb would be to consider whether there is any benefit in converting the previous 12 months of data. Anything more than 12 months and the time and cost involved is likely to far outweigh any benefits.

Options for conversion - do it yourself, get an expert to convert

In some cases you may have a few options on how to convert the data. One of course, is to do it yourself. This is not recommended unless you have a good understanding of accounting principles and the expertise to learn and understand a new system quickly. The better option is to get your accountant to undertake the conversion, or find a conversion expert for the particular system you are going to use and hire them to undertake the work for you. You will save a mountain of time, stress and frustration by arranging for someone else to do this work for you and it will be worth every penny it may cost you.

Having said that, the cost of conversion should be fairly reasonable and you should not feel that it is expensive.

Summary

1   It is worth spending time and money to be trained properly on the use of the cloud accounting system you choose.

2   If you know how to use the system properly you will get much better information from it and will learn the short cuts and tricks and tips from experts who use the system regularly.

3   Conversion of data from the old system can usually be done quite simply by an experienced bookkeeper or accountant, or by industry specialists in conversion of data.

Chapter 7

Different cloud accounting systems available

There are far too many different cloud accounting systems currently available to mention them all. In fact, every day there are new systems popping up.

The available cloud accounting systems can be grouped into a few different categories.

Personal finance systems. These systems are not suitable for your business. However, they are really great for keeping track of your personal income and spending. Some of these systems allow you to plan a budget for the year and keep track of how your personal spending is compared to your planned budget. If you are saving for a home deposit, wanting to invest money regularly, needing to make sure you have enough money for the kids' education or for your annual vacation, then these systems are perfect.

But, don't try and use them to run your business; no matter how small that business is. **Examples of these systems are – Mint.com, Personal Xero.**

Invoicing systems. These systems are not in fact accounting systems. They are designed specifically to allow you to invoice your customers or clients. You will be able to keep track of who has paid you, who hasn't and follow-up on outstanding invoices. However, these systems are not accounting systems and will not provide you with the full accounting records your accountant will need. **Examples of these systems are – Bill.com and FreshBooks.**

Partial accounting systems. These systems look a bit like accounting systems, but are not based on proper accounting principles. They will be missing certain functions which are necessary to be full accounting systems. This may be a chart of accounts, or the ability to input manual journal entries (accounting jargon), but without them you will be severely limited in the use of the system and they are unlikely to provide you with the reporting capability you need for your business. **Example – LessAccounting.**

Full accounting systems. These are the bigger players. They tend to be better known and will have wider acceptance by your accountant. Every accountant will have their favourite cloud accounting system, just as they have had their favourite desktop software over the past decades. Some accountants may be happy working with a couple of different systems acknowledging there isn't really a one size fits all product which suits different types of business. However, most accountants will be specialist users with one system and have working knowledge of perhaps another one or two.

Within the full cloud accounting systems options there are two distinct types. The first is the accounting system which provides purely an accounting solution. This type of system will not integrate with other systems you may use in your business, for example your CRM or eCommerce platform. **Example – MYOB LiveAccounts.**

The other type of cloud accounting system is one which integrates with other systems – from CRM, inventory, Point of Sale, eCommerce, Project Management and Time Tracking to name a few. To ensure your business uses the best options for future growth and expansion, or simply for future efficiencies, these types of systems are the most favourable pick. You may not use any of the other systems that integrate with your accounting system to start with, but over time I am sure you will find the need to use other systems and see the benefits of having them all integrate and "talk" to each other.

Just think of the time saving that can be gained from using something like, SalesForce, a program that allows you to have the details of your prospects and leads automatically integrated into your accounting system so when you need to invoice your customers or clients, their details are already there. **Examples of these systems are – Xero, e-Conomics.**

To give you some perspective of the different cloud accounting systems I have summarised six of the systems currently available.

XERO – Beautiful Accounting Software

Xero was founded in 2006 and is a publicly listed company on both the Australian and New Zealand Stock Exchanges. Xero has offices and users all over the world including New Zealand, Australia, the USA and the UK. At the time of printing, after just six years, Xero has over 135,000 business owners around the world using the system and this number is growing exponentially. With major shareholders with large pockets, Xero has the financial viability to continue to grow both with numbers of users and also with enhancements to the Xero system.

At the time of writing, Xero is the leader in cloud accounting systems in New Zealand and Australia. Their goal is for the system to be global; the markets they are currently concentrating on are the USA and the UK.

Xero releases new features and enhancements based on feedback and suggestions from their customers every three to six weeks. Thus the system is continually evolving and improving. Some of these enhancements are minor tweaks, whilst others are major changes which significantly improve the way you can operate your business using Xero.

Xero has identified the top ten reasons why their customers love Xero:

1 Automated daily bank feeds.
2 Fast, simple and customised invoicing.
3 Available anytime you're online, from anywhere.
4 Work together as a team on financials.
5 Safe and secure.
6 Smart reports with quick links to the source transaction.
7 Dashboard gives a clear financial overview.
8 Awesome support at no additional cost.
9 No installation or IT maintenance required.
10 Pay as you go and no up-front costs.

Xero has a mobile app which can be used on your iPhone or Android to allow you to check out your accounts when you are out and about. You can also create and send invoices from the mobile app which is great if you are a tradesman or sales person as you can do this on the spot with the customer or client, rather than waiting until you are back in the office to produce the invoice. With the availability of credit card processing from mobile phones (or the mobile credit card machines), this can mean invoicing and being paid on the spot. No more doing the invoices late at night and then having to chase your customers to get paid.

Xero is easy to learn even if you don't have an accounting or bookkeeping background. It is simple and a pleasure to use.

Xero was the first cloud accounting system to link bank statement data directly into the accounting system and now has full daily bank data feed integration with over 600 banks and financial institutions worldwide including PayPal. If you are using PayPal for your business, it is important you check whether the system you are intending to use has the integration. Manually treating PayPal transactions can be very time consuming, particularly if you have a high volume of transactions of similar value.

A large part of the success story of Xero is the way they have allowed other developers to write other systems which integrate with Xero. These are called add-ons. This means that as your business expands, and your need for further systems increases, you are able to find a system which will integrate with Xero. No more multiple databases, no more entering information in two or more places.

There are add-ons available for specific industries with different requirements – e.g. medical practitioners, lawyers, tradesmen – which have been written to provide the structure to process your business information and integrate this with your accounting system.

Like most of these systems, Xero has a dashboard which shows you your bank balances, whether they are reconciled and if not, how many transactions need to be reconciled, your accounts receivable and accounts payable, and any expense claims. In addition, you are able to add a number of line items to the dashboard so you can keep track of specific figures easily every time you log into the system. You might want to keep an eye on your income, or the amount you owe the tax man, or there may be specific expense items which you want to watch. These line items can be changed at any time which allows you the flexibility to change them as your business requirements change. You may find you need to keep a watch on your advertising costs for a period of time and then, when you are comfortable that this is running according to your budget and needs; you might change to keeping a watch on your employment costs.

Xero does all of the standard accounting functions: bank reconciliations, invoicing and accounts receivable, expenses and accounts payable.

In addition, if you have transactions or bank accounts in different currencies, Xero works with 160 different currencies and will automatically calculate any exchange gains or losses due to fluctuations in the exchange rates. The exchange rates are updated hourly within Xero.

The reports are able to be produced using your local currency or in a foreign currency.

Xero has payroll integrated in some countries. The system allows you to provide your employees with access to their own payroll details. In this way, they can enter their working hours, request leave and view their payslips. So, if your employee loses a payslip or wants to double check what their leave entitlements are, they are able to login themselves to check their own details. This is great for your staff and also a time saver for the person in your business who looks after the payroll as they won't need to be answering these types of questions anymore or chasing up staff for their hours worked.

If you are in the building and construction industry in Australia, you are required to provide a summary of payments to any sub-contractors after the end of each year. Xero allows you to easily keep track of these payments by using the categories function when paying the sub-contractors.

Your accountant will be happy if you are using Xero as the system allows for depreciation calculations to be prepared within Xero. In most cases, this is a function which your accountant would usually undertake and you will need the highest user rights to access this. However, it does allow for the depreciation charges to be calculated monthly, thus improving the accuracy of your monthly reports.

Xero has budgeting capability built-in and reports which allow you to check how you are going against your forecast. This is a vital report for any business to ensure the goals established at the beginning of the year are being focused on. Any variation from the forecast/budget can then be reviewed and corrective action taken.

One of the major accounting components which Xero does not have built-in is a full inventory system. Xero itself allows for the use of inventory items which means you can keep track of these and include the items on invoicing. However, it does not keep track of the stock numbers or reporting. To obtain this you need to also subscribe to one of the add-ons which is specifically written for inventory.

Xero has over 40 reports within the system which can be simply prepared.

E-Conomics

e-Conomics commenced in 2001 and at the time of printing has over 94,000 businesses using the system throughout Europe and in over 50 countries around the world. The company began in Denmark and has spread with offices in eight countries in Europe. e-Conomics is available in nine European languages.

e-Conomics has a history similar to Xero and is the market leader for small business online accounting systems usage in Europe, where Xero is currently the market leader in Australia and New Zealand. Both have goals of spreading worldwide.

e-Conomics has a full general ledger, accounts receivable and accounts payable functions together with invoicing. The system does not include inventory or payroll.

Due to the fact that e-Conomics has been established in Europe with expansion capability around the world, the system allows for multiple currencies and daily exchange rate updates. The system will automatically calculate Valued Added Tax (VAT) requirements.

Bank integration is available to reduce the data entry for the bank account transactions.

Inventory and stock control are an example of add-on systems offered. There are many other add-on systems available for your business needs to allow for extra functionality or business growth and specific items needed for your business. e-Conomics has a mobile app which is available for iPhones, iPads, Android smartphones and tablets allowing even more flexibility in your ability to access your financial information when you want to and to undertake invoicing and other functions wherever you may be.

MYOB Live Accounts and MYOB AccountRight Live Plus

MYOB has recently released their online options. There are basically two options. For small business with no inventory and a simple payroll, the solution is MYOB Live Accounts.

LiveAccounts has a dashboard which shows bank balances, how much money your customers or clients owe you. It also has a feature which is really practical for Australian and New Zealand businesses, which is that it shows how much money you owe for your GST and PAYG Withholding. This is ever more important as the tax man is taking the view that the money you collect for GST from your sales is their money and not yours. Similarly, the tax you deduct from your employees wages each payday is the tax man's money and not yours. As such you must not use this money for paying your bills, but rather you should have it in your bank account at all times ready to pay to the tax man when it is due.

MYOB states that:

" LiveAccounts is purpose built for people new

to accounting or accounting software."

This is a fully online system but with limited reporting and functionality.

The second MYOB option is AccountRight Live Plus which is being promoted with a choice of storing your data on your desktop or on the cloud. This is, in fact, a hybrid system. A true cloud system has everything – the system and the data – in the cloud. MYOB AccountRight Live Plus only has your business data in the cloud. You still need to have software on your computer. This does solve the issue of the data being on one computer where you are responsible for making sure it is backed up regularly. In the event that there is a disaster with your computer, you would need to revert to the most recent back-up you have.

The need to have software on your computer though, does mean this system has some restrictions. MYOB AccountRightLiveAccounts won't allow you to login from just any computer to access your business data. As long as you have your own computer device and internet access with you, then you will have access to your data. Consequently, if you want your bookkeeper and your accountant to have access to your data, they must have MYOB software installed on their computers to do so.

MYOB AccountRightLiveAccounts has three versions with the top one including full inventory, time based billing and payroll functionality.

MYOB AccountRightLiveAccounts has bank data feeds for 100 financial institutions in Australia and New Zealand. Currently, if you are not an Australian or New Zealand based business, this system will not work for you.

SAASU online accounting

Saasu was one of the earliest online accounting systems and has been in operation for over 10 years. Saasu currently has more than 20,000 businesses using the system in the Asia Pacific region. Xero has overtaken

Saasu as the market leader in Australia and New Zealand despite only being in operation for six years, due in part to the additional financial resources Xero has available, and also the expertise of the people.

Saasu has offices in Australia, New Zealand and the UK.

Saasu has a number of different features, including the ability to create your own dashboard with the financial figures which are most important to you. Whilst most businesses have similar key financial figures which should be on a dashboard, if you have a business which is a bit different to the standard, this feature allows you to put those other key financial figures on your dashboard.

Saasu has automated daily bank feeds and easy reconciliation processes. If your bank account is not able to be part of the automated bank feeds, you can manually import the bank statement data from your internet banking which is fine; however, this does take more time and effort compared to the automated bank feeds. Saasu has full integration with PayPal which not all systems have. Saasu promotes that it has "comprehensive invoicing workflow." The invoicing system, like most others, allows you to customise your invoice with your logo and prepare sophisticated invoices. Invoices can be emailed directly to your customer or client and the usual reporting functions are available to identify which customers or clients you need to chase for payment. The system allows you to prepare quotes and attach other documents to invoices, e.g. warranty documents.

The system also allows you to create recurring invoices and for these to be automatically created.

Saasu has full inventory built into the system. This includes keeping track of stock numbers, being able to set alerts so you know when to order more stock when the stock is below your pre-determined minimum level. There is integrated functionality with e-commerce systems and the system will update with integration from eBay and TradeMe.

Saasu supports multiple currencies with foreign currency accounts for 50 different currencies. The system will update exchange rates on a daily basis.

Saasu also includes in the system a Customer Relationship Management (CRM) system. The system allows you to manage correspondence with your customers or clients, keep track of potential sales and marketing campaigns.

With many different connectors or add-ons, the system can expand to suit your needs. Saasu has added their own in SaasuPOS – which is a point of sale system which has particular application to the hospitality industry.

QuickBooks online – US version

QuickBooks desktop software was first released in 1984 and the company released their online accounting system in 2001. The statement on their website is, "QuickBooks is more than secure online accounting. It's your business organised in one place."

QuickBooks desktop software is difficult to comprehend without some bookkeeping or accounting knowledge. The online system similarly requires some prior knowledge of the desktop QuickBooks software, bookkeeping or accounting. If you are using QuickBooks in your business, you will find the online version simple to follow.

QuickBooks Online – the US Version is the full version of the system and has a significant base of users in the US with full functionality for US taxes and forms and possibly has the greatest market share of US small business users. In 2011, QuickBooks Online had 215,000 subscribers.

QuickBooks Online includes general ledger, accounts receivable, accounts payable, inventory, and payroll for employees and contractors, connection to bank accounts and credit cards. QuickBooks Online provides a company snapshot scorecard to provide you a summary of the business at a glance.

You can access QuickBooks Online from your iPhone, BlackBerry or Android. Like all the online systems, the data is secure and backed-up by the system automatically.

The system provides access to over 60 different financial reports to stay on top of your business.

QuickBooks online – non US version

At the time of printing, this is the poor cousin version compared to the US version of QuickBooks Online. Due to different taxes in different countries, the non US version does not include payroll or inventory. In addition, some of the add-ons are not available and some of the other must have features are not included in this version.

Others

There are a myriad of other online accounting systems, too many to mention and with more being introduced every day.

For information about currently available systems visit: *www.connectedtechnologybook.com/resources/systems*

Chapter 8

Integration with other business systems

After making the decision to move to a cloud accounting system, the next step is to decide which one of the myriad of options is the best for you and your business. There are no right or wrong decisions and the decisions will be based on a number of factors, many of which have been discussed previously.

One of the keys to running an efficient business is to have one system which integrates all the different parts of the business into one central location. How much time do you spend entering the same data over and over again into a CRM system, current customer or client database and also your accounting system? Wouldn't it be great to have a system where the information is entered once and it automatically updates all the relevant databases for you? Well, now you can. This is one of the biggest benefits of the more advanced cloud accounting systems. The systems have been designed in such a way by computer savvy developers that you only need one database to integrate with all of your programs.

You need to have a good hard look at your business. What systems are you currently using, what systems would you like to have in a perfect world, what could you do differently if you had integrated systems? When you have a list of the types of systems you need, you can then review what options are available to you.

For example, you might be using SalesForce to keep records of your potential customers or clients and to track the performance of your sales people. You might be using a spreadsheet to control when the work commences and when the job is completed. And then you would have an accounting system from which you issue invoices and keep the overall accounting records. With the right cloud accounting system, you would be able to have all the information about your potential customers or leads, the work in progress, the invoicing and all the other accounting functions all integrating with each other.

Client relationship management (CRM)

CRM systems have been available for many years and in most cases are stand alone programs which are used by sales people. These keep track of potential customers or clients; they may record notes on phone calls, emails and meetings. The program may also include details of quotes, reactions to the quote, amended quotes and ultimately, when the quote is approved, the system is updated to confirm the prospect is now a customer or client. At that point for a lot of the systems, those details are then archived and not referred to again. The sales person moves on to the next sale and so on.

The benefit of integration of the CRM system with a cloud accounting system is there is no need to re-enter the basic data. An integrated CRM will automatically convert the quote into either a job or an invoice when the quote is accepted. Another benefit of the integration is you never have to worry again about keeping track of the approved quotes and whether you have missed one.

Booking systems

Does your business provide services which require booking appointments? There are a number of cloud booking systems available which will allow you to make appointments, and some even allow your customers to make the appointment themselves for the time and day that suits them best (based on your availability). There are a number of benefits to having a booking system which integrates with your accounting system. Firstly, as with so many other integrated systems, it removes the need for you to enter the basic data about your customers or clients multiple times. Secondly, it is a great way to keep track of your appointments and the income from each appointment. Thirdly, the integration is an excellent management tool to ensure that all income is recorded properly and where you have different employees, it can keep track of the income each of them is earning for the business in an efficient manner. This is particularly useful if you pay your employees based on the work they have done, or there is a bonus system or they get paid a percentage of the income they generate.

Using a Booking System to Calculate Employee Entitlements

Michelle is a chiropractor with multiple business premises. She has qualified chiropractors who work from the different premises and pay a portion of their income to cover the costs of rent, electricity, supplies, administration staff and so on.

Michelle used to have handwritten daily booking sheets which would show each of the customers' names and what services they had. The total amount charged to the customer was then entered onto the booking sheet when the customer paid at the end of their treatment. Michelle used to tally up the totals for each chiropractor at the end of the week to calculate the amount which they owed her. This would take Michelle a couple of hours to do and there was always the chance that she added it up wrong. As a result, she would add the figures two and three times to make sure that the figures were correct.

Michelle came to see me seeking advice on how to process these figures more efficiently. We recommended that she establisha cloud accounting system with an integrated bookkeeping system. The customers love the system as they can book their appointments at any time of the day or night online.

> *Michelle loves the system as now she can simply produce a report at the end of the week and it identifies exactly how much income each of the chiropractors has brought into the business and Michelle can then easily calculate their entitlement and make the payments. She has saved herself roughly three hours of calculations each week.*

Debt collection

If you are like most business owners, getting paid can be a major challenge and a big frustration. Traditionally, you would be issuing invoices when you have completed work, or sold an item. In many cases you will have offered 30 days credit without even checking out the customer or client first and then at the end of the month you go into your accounting software system and print out statements which you mail to your customers or clients and hope this will remind them to pay you.

Unfortunately in today's world of fast-speed everything, a statement doesn't provide the best call to action to make your customer or client pay you. There are add-on systems in cloud accounting systems which will automate the process by sending out emails on a weekly basis based on who still owes you money. These systems integrate with the accounting system and thus only send out reminder emails to those people who owe you money.

The business who gets paid first is often the one who makes contact the most frequently. At the end of the day the person receiving the emails – and you should follow up from time to time with a phone call too – will get sick and tired of receiving them and pay you just to stop the onslaught.

With this process considerably automated it doesn't need to take up much of your time and the result should be more money in your bank account quicker.

Time tracking

Where your business is based on billing the time taken to complete each job, the time tracking systems will keep a record of the time spent by each employee on the jobs. These systems are a great way of managing staff, whether they are in or away from the business premises doing work. For example, if you have a business with a number of tradesmen who are doing a number of jobs in a day, the time tracking can record how much time each job has taken. This makes it much easier for you or your bookkeeper to invoice each of the jobs for the correct charges based on the right amount of hours.

Again, like so many of these systems, the integration of the time tracking with the cloud accounting system will eliminate the need for you to enter the customer or clients' data into two systems.

Point of sale

One of the most important functions of any retail business is recording the sales to the customer at the time of sale whilst the customer is in the business premises and providing them with a receipt for the goods or services. Point of Sale (POS) systems historically have been simply a cash register system which records the sales and potentially has the ability to produce a report at the end of the day to show your sales. Sometimes this is as simple as the Z total report from the till. Some of the POS systems also have a form of inventory system within them and may provide reports showing the stock-on -hand figures.

Furthermore, there are POS systems which integrate with accounting desktop software systems. If you are using one of these systems, the chances are you are paying a reasonably high price for your software and the annual support fees. These integrated desktop systems provide all the relevant integration and reporting in relation to stock items sold, stock-on-hand and reports for stock re-ordering.

The benefit of a POS using a cloud based system is the cost of the system is usually significantly less than the desktop software. The integration with the cloud accounting system provides all the information you require to keep control over your inventory. In some businesses, you will have sales at the counter which may be lay-bys, or for account customers who will pay at the end of the month. These sales in an integrated system will be properly recorded and you will be able to keep track of these very easily.

Integration of a POS system with
an accounting system

Mike was referred to me by a colleague after he split from his business partner who was responsible for the accounting side of the business. His business consisted of retail shop selling swimming pool supplies and a service division for servicing pools in the local area. We found the accounting in a mess. The business partner ran the retail shop and had been responsible for the bookkeeping of the business whilst Mike undertook the service calls. However, no bookkeeping had been done. There was a POS system which was being used in the shop, but Mike didn't know anything more than how to use the cash register component of it and the rest of the system was not up to date, nor were we able to obtain any useful reports from it.

The biggest challenges facing Mike was he had no idea how much stock he had in the shop, the sale prices weren't up to date and he felt he had no control over the business at all. It was obvious we needed to install a POS system with inventory and link it to the accounting system to minimise the data entry and bookkeeping time.

We found a good POS system which integrated with the cloud accounting system and proceeded to install the two simultaneously. This necessitated a full stock take to be done so we had the correct starting point. Mike also needed to update his sales prices.

We installed the new system before the busy summer season and Mike is now benefiting from having more control over the system. He knows exactly what is in stock, he is able to see how much profit he is making and can keep track of the business. He has employed a retail shop assistant who is able to operate the POS system whilst Mike continues to attend to the service side of the business. At any time during the day, Mike is able to access the system and check the trading results from the retail side.

Ecommerce

Even before cloud accounting systems had become prevalent; selling through the internet had taken hold. You may already be selling your products or services through your website, through an eBay store or even through an event booking system. There are a number of eCommerce solutions which are available to keep track of sales through your website and integrate seamlessly into cloud accounting systems. For many years, this was not an option; instead you had to enter the sales from your website manually as the money showed up in your bank account. If you were selling both through the internet and through a bricks and mortar shop, it was often difficult for you to track how much was sold through each location and to obtain useful reports which separated the two.

The correct ecommerce system will seamlessly integrate with your cloud accounting system and your inventory system too.

Project management

Many businesses calculate the invoice amount of their customers or clients using a combination of time based billing and charges for external costs. These types of businesses typically keep track of the work on a job by job basis and use spreadsheets to keep track of this information. If you are in a service type business, you will have some kind of project management requirements. Integrated project management systems allow all this information to be recorded in both the project management system and the accounting system to keep track of costs to date on the projects, costs incurred, data about the customer or client, the quote for the project, invoices issued relating to the project and profit or loss on the job. The relevant figures for costs and invoiced amounts are fed through to the accounting system, thus removing the need to enter this information twice.

Keeping track of staff on the road

Similar to project management and time tracking, there are now systems which you can use to keep track of your staff that are out of the office. These systems keep track of what they are doing through the day. This not only ensures all their time is charged to a customer or client, but it also holds them more accountable for their movements and work during the day.

Do you have staff who work out of the office or away from the business premises? Do you know where they are throughout the day? Do you know exactly how much time they have taken to complete each job? Are you sure they haven't taken two hours for lunch or gone home early? These questions can be answered, and the staff managed more successfully with a system which keeps track of the location of your staff throughout the day. These systems work by tracking the vehicle or mobile device via GPS and then using this information to complete real time job sheets based on the time at the location. A further advantage of these systems is being able to allocate jobs to those employees nearest to the job. Some of these systems allow you to message your employees and send them the job details instantly. No need to waste time on phone calls.

Industry specific

As more and more web developers are writing systems, there are more specific cloud systems which are becoming available. Most of these are industry specific. For example, there is a system specially written for lawyers for their trust accounting, there is one in Australia specifically for doctors allowing for automatic processing of Medicare claims on the spot whilst the patient is in the surgery and for those claims to be reconciled when paid.

Before making a decision on which cloud accounting system to use, check whether there are any industry specific options available for your business. The benefits of these add-ons can be massive in ease of use, time saving efficiencies, reporting and control.

Not for profits

Are you working in or running a not for profit organisation? There are many benefits to be gained from using cloud accounting systems. You will have many different volunteers who will be working within the organisation. Some will be specifically looking after the bookkeeping functions. Some may be involved in invoicing and keeping track of the money coming in. Others again may be running a specific fundraising function and need to enter the information and manage the financial aspects of that particular part of the operation. The benefit of using a cloud accounting system is the ability for many different people who are involved to have access to the same financial data at anytime, anywhere they may be, simultaneously or not and do whatever part of the work they need to do at a convenient time.

Cloud accounting systems are generally fairly easy to learn which also helps when you are dealing with volunteers entering data into the system and reconciling, chasing up outstanding payments and so on. When one volunteer leaves, another is able to pick-up the work to be done and take over without spending hours learning a program like you had to with desktop accounting software. With desktop accounting software, you needed to have a volunteer who had bookkeeping or accounting knowledge, and preferably one who knew how to use the accounting software the not for profit was using. This is no longer necessary, due to the ease of the learning process.

Summary

1   Review the add-ons available with the cloud accounting system you are proposing to use.

2   Consider the future growth of your business and what other requirements you may have in the future.

3   Check whether any of the add-ons are stand alone systems which you may already be using in your business.

4   For those add-ons which you need from the get go, find out more information about them before you make a decision.

5   Check whether there are any industry specific systems for your business.

Chapter 9

How to choose the right cloud accounting system for your business

17 Questions you need to ask

What type of business are you in?

This is a fundamental question which will point you in the direction of the correct cloud accounting system for you. Are you a retail business, a service business, a graphic designer, a tradesman, a manufacturer, a catering contractor, a doctor or dentist? Do you sell your products or services to other businesses or to the public? Are you a business with a large number of staff or are you a one person business? Do you have lots of small transactions, or do you have a few large value transactions in your business? The more you understand exactly what your business does and its needs, the easier it will be to determine the right cloud accounting solution.

What country do you operate your business from and pay taxes in?

This is an important question as every country has different tax requirements. Basic bookkeeping will be the same irrespective of where you work in the world. However, the tax requirements will be different for every country. Some systems will have the right taxes built into the system for you and others won't.

Do you use multiple currencies?

Whether you buy products or services or sell them, if you deal with currencies other than your local currency you may find the use of a cloud accounting system will provide time saving currency conversions which are automatically processed.

What type of invoicing do you require?

Do you issue invoices to your customers or clients? Are these regular or ad-hoc? Do you have standard invoices where your customers or clients pay a set amount, or does every invoice contain different details? Do you have more than one trading name for your business and need different invoices to reflect this? Flexibility in the format of the invoice may be an important factor in the decision. However, if you have standard invoices then flexibility may not matter.

Do you have inventory and need stock control?

If your business sells products and you need to keep track of how many you have on hand, when you need to re-order more in, and a multitude of other reporting requirements to keep track of your inventory, then you will find this information may require you to use an add-on to the cloud accounting system as many of the systems currently do not have this level of functionality built into the system. A thorough review of what the cloud accounting system does or doesn't do will determine whether you will require an add-on and which add-on will be best for your business. These add-on systems are best for wholesalers and warehouses where the stock is sold in bulk to other businesses and not sold to the public on the spot.

Do you have a retail outlet and require a Point of Sale (POS) system?

Retail businesses, whether you are a store selling products or a restaurant, you will need to capture and process the sale whilst your customer is on the premises together with collecting payment, whether it is cash or credit card. In this case you will require a POS system and one that integrates seamlessly with your cloud accounting system. Some POS systems have been designed specifically with restaurants and cafes in mind, others for retail stores selling products. These systems will typically also have inventory and stock control included in them.

Do you sell online?

The advent of selling online has taken hold and people from around the world will buy products from an online store. There are no country boundaries other than those relating to shipping restrictions. Your online store sales must integrate with your cloud accounting system to save doubling up on data entry and to ensure your stock levels are correctly maintained. The online selling systems are similar to the POS systems except they integrate with the shopping cart on your website.

Do you require time management or project management systems?

Do you invoice your customers or clients for work done and charge by the hour? If so, then you need to look into the time management solutions to integrate your time charges into your cloud accounting system.

Do you undertake project work where some of your invoice will be based on hours worked, and some on outside costs? Then you need to look into the project management systems to find one which will suit your requirements.

Integration of both time management and project management systems will provide a major improvement in the reporting of this part of your business.

Are you in an industry requiring specialised systems?

There are systems available which have been written for specific industries. In Australia, there have been a number written as add-ons to Xero, for example. One has been written for businesses in the legal profession, another for doctors to allow them to bulk bill part of their fees directly to the government through the system. If you have specific requirements, check and see what is available for your industry.

Do you employ staff and need payroll functions?

Not all cloud accounting systems have the payroll functions built into their systems. This is partly to allow for the system to be used in different countries which leaves you to either find an add-on for the payroll in your country or to do the payroll separately from the account-ing system. Make sure if there is a payroll function that it does comply with your local payroll tax requirements.

Do you need to keep track of leads and sales generation?

Customer Relationship Management (CRM) systems have been available for some period of time and these will help you keep track of your potential customers, follow up on the leads and report on the sales conversion. When you have an integrated CRM system with a cloud accounting system you won't need to re-enter basic information more than once. An integrated CRM will also automatically convert a quote into either a job or an invoice depending upon what type of business you are in when the quote is accepted. Another benefit of the integration is you never have to worry again about keeping track of the approved quotes and whether you have missed one.

CRM systems are vital if your business is marketing for new business and has one or more sales people who are meeting with your prospects to make sales.

What system do you use to keep in contact with your customers or clients?

An integrated system which allows you to have your customers or clients email addresses and mailing addresses linked to your automated email system will eliminate duplication of entry of information and ensure your automated email system will always be up to date.

Do you need to have access to your accounting system whilst you are away from your business premises?

If you travel often in your business then it is important the cloud accounting system you choose has a mobile app to provide access to your records via your mobile device —whether a Smartphone, iPad, or tablet.

What support and help is provided?

Every cloud accounting system has some level of support, from help sections with minimal information to help sections with very detailed information, screenshot instructions, and videos along with email support with online chat options. If you are new to business or new to the bookkeeping functions, a system with detailed support will be essential.

Who will be completing the bookkeeping work?

Will you be doing the bookkeeping work yourself, will you employ a bookkeeper or will your accountant be assisting with this function? This will help determine the level of different access requirements you will need and also the amount of training and support.

What is the price of the system?

Every system is priced slightly differently. Some systems, as noted previously, have more functions built into the systems, others have less and you will need to also pay for the add-ons. However, cloud accounting systems are generally cheaper than the mainstream desktop software systems from the past. The main difference is there isn't an up-front cost to establish a cloud accounting system. There are some "free" cloud accounting systems, but these are free due to advertising rights which means each time you access your accounting records you will have advertising on your screen. The downside to most of the free systems is they don't provide the functionality you should have for your business.

What system does your accountant use and support?

This is a very important consideration and may in fact lead you to change accountants. It is imperative your accountant is familiar with the system you are using. If your accountant understands all of the functions and abilities of the system they will be better able to provide information and advice to you about your business. In addition, if your accountant knows the system, they will be able to answer some of the how to questions which will arise along the way.

Identifying Business Requirements

Bill is a dentist with a well established business. He was unhappy with his existing bookkeeping processes and sought advice on how it could be improved. After going through the 17 questions we determined that he needed a system which would integrate his accounting system with a booking system for his appointments and a CRM with emailing capabilities. He also needed an invoicing system with item numbers for claims from health funds, an integrated payroll, an email system for automated reminders, automated supplier invoice processing, and he also needed a pseudo point of sale component for his staff to use for processing invoices and receiving payments. With the list of requirements determined, I was able to recommend an integrated solution for his business. He now has full control over the business and has seen improved productivity from his administration staff too.

Summary

1 Take a good look at your business and the
information you require now and may require
in the future.

2 Consider what other systems you need to integrate.

3 Review alternatives before making a decision.

4 Check out what others are saying about the system.

5 Ask your peers whether they are using a cloud
accounting system and if so, which one and whether
they are happy with it.

6 Obtain independent advice to help make
the decision.

7 Check out forums and reviews online.

Chapter 10

Reporting

Dashboards - summarised main items on one page with graphical display

As I discussed in Chapter 4 one of the benefits of most cloud accounting systems is the dashboard. This is usually the first screen you see when you log into your cloud accounting system. Each system will have a slightly different dashboard. However, generally most will show the balance in your bank account(s), the balance owing to you by your customers or clients (accounts receivable or debtors), and the amount you owe suppliers (accounts payable or creditors).

The dashboard will often show the figures in graphical form which you may find easier to understand than a series of numbers.

Financial reports

Within the better cloud accounting systems, there will be many different reports available for you to screen and print. As a business owner, you do need to understand the fundamentals of each of these reports. You will find over time that the more you look at these reports, and particularly if you review these with your accountant, the more you will understand them and in turn understand how well your business is running.

Trading statement

The *trading statement* shows the income less the direct costs. Direct costs are typically the cost of an item stocked and freight costs to get the item to you from the manufacturer or wholesaler. If you are selling time, then direct costs will include the cost of labour for those employees who produced the income. These costs include wages, superannuation and vehicle expenses.

The trading statement will take into account any stock you have on hand at the date of the report. The income less all the direct costs equals the *gross profit margin* for the period. It is important to look at this figure as a percentage of the total income.

Profit and loss statement

The *profit and loss statement* shows the gross profit margin from the trading statement as income together with any other sundry income, e.g. interest received, and then lists all the overhead costs of the business for the period. Overhead costs are generally expenses which need to be paid no matter how many sales you make or how much income you earn. For example, rent of the business premises has to be paid each month no matter the circumstances. Other overhead costs are bank charges, employment costs of administration staff, printing and stationery, bank fees, accounting and legal fees, subscriptions and licenses, electricity, telephone, travel costs and many others. The profit and loss includes the income from sales you have made to customers who haven't paid you yet, and expenses which you have made, but haven't yet paid to your suppliers.

Balance sheet

For most, this is the report which you are least likely to understand in the early days of your business. The balance sheet is a snapshot of your financial position at a particular point in time. It shows you how much money you have in the bank, how much money your customers or clients owe you, how much money you have spent on purchasing equipment, machinery, furniture, vehicles and assets with the life span of more than a year. It also shows you how much money you owe to your suppliers, the tax man, the bank if you have borrowed money for the business or have a bank overdraft account, and how much money the business owes you if you used some of your own personal money to start the business.

Cashflow statement

This statement is often confused with the profit and loss statement. If you are like most people when you first go into business, you won't have an extensive knowledge of financial reports and what they mean. You will start off simply looking at how much money has come into your bank account and how much money has gone out of it. You will then see how much is left for you. This is the measuring stick novice business owners will use to decide if they are profitable or not. This calculation is effectively what a *cashflow statement* will show you. It is a summary of what money has been deposited into your bank account and where it came from (this may include money you lent to the business to get it started or to pay bills when there wasn't enough money in the bank account to do so, in addition to sales receipts) and what money has been paid out of the bank account (this may include costs of buying equipment, paying back money lent to the business in addition to the payment of the expenses of running the business).

However, it is important to understand that this is not necessarily a true reflection of whether the business is really making a profit or not. Only the profit and loss statement will show these figures correctly.

Accounts receivable or debtors report

The accounts receivable report shows the amounts owing to you by your customers or clients and will show the amounts due which were invoiced in the current month, those outstanding more than 30 days, more than 60 days and those 90 days or more. This report is vital to keep track of money that is owing to you and to chase up your customers or clients to make sure you get paid for the goods you sold or the services you have provided.

Accounts payable or creditors report

The accounts payable report shows the amounts you owe to your suppliers. This report like the accounts receivable report will split the amounts owing into current costs, those owing for 30 days, those owing for 60 days and those owing for more than 90 days.

Tax due reports

Depending on which country you live in, you will need to be looking at the *Tax Due Reports* which will show the amounts you owe to the tax man for GST, VAT, Sales Tax, State Taxes and Federal Taxes. In most countries the tax man considers the taxes you collect as part of your sales price is not your money to use as you are collecting that money on behalf of the tax man. It is thus important that you always know how much money you owe to the tax man.

For examples of these reports go to *www.connected technology book.com/resources/reports*

***Quarterly review meeting uncovers plans for
future direction and identification of cashflow
requirements***

*Dianne is in the business of web hosting and web
development and has been running her business for a
few years. The turnover has been low and she hasn't
been making any money. Dianne decided to use a cloud
accounting system at the beginning of the previous
year and was using the figures purely for reporting
purposes for the tax man. Her main reporting was
from her CRM system which had all the details of her
customers, the amounts owed and for which services.
Dianne's previous accountant only completed the
annual compliance work and recommended she deal
with her GST on an annual basis.*

*A review of the first quarter's trading results
showed the income of the business had increased
significantly during the last two months of the
quarter; she had employed a full-time person to assist
with specific aspects of the business and ceased
using the services of a part-time contractor. Dianne
had outstanding tax debts from prior years and was
paying those debts off with monthly instalments.*

*Two key factors came to light in the course of the
quarterly meeting. Firstly, a new GST liability was*

highlighted which needed to be paid in full within a few weeks. Dianne had drawn funds from the business which needed to be treated as wages and the appropriate amount of tax calculated for payment to the tax man.

I recommended that the GST components be paid quarterly based on the correct figures from the trading, rather than either paying an estimate for the quarter or paying the amount annually. It is always easier on cashflow to pay a little bit each month or quarter than it is to find a large lump sum of money after the end of the year. We discussed the need to also put money aside to make sure she has sufficient funds to pay the next quarterly amount due 13 weeks later. I estimated the amount of tax liabilities, wages liabilities, and superannuation and recommended that she transfer $1/13^{th}$ of the amount into a separate bank account every week to make sure that she has the funds available.

The second factor that came to light related to the source of income. We discussed in more detail exactly what type of work she does and where the income comes from. Through her CRM system she determined there were two main sources of income for the business, one which is a regular monthly income stream which has been building steadily over the years from referrals. The second type of income *is project based. We then discussed marketing plans for both of her income streams.*

After the meeting was concluded, Dianne said that it was the best meeting she had ever had with an accountant. In the past she had never received any advice or recommendations relating to the payment of taxes and the need to review the reports to keep track of the taxes due.

Reporting on key performance indicators (KPI's)

Key performance indicators are simply a fancy name for the important numbers in your business. Sometimes they are percentages, number of days or amounts. In every case they tell the story of how well or poorly your business is running. Key performance indicators or KPI's can be specific to your business or your industry, or they can be more general making them relevant for all types of businesses.

The most common general KPI's

Accounts Receivable Days – this shows the average number of days it takes your customers or clients to pay your invoices. The smaller the number of days are;

the better. If you have a retail business, then this KPI will not be relevant for you as you get paid at the time of sale except if you provide a layby service. However, for many businesses, you will be selling your goods or services on credit. Meaning you allow your customers or clients to pay you at some time in the future. You may extend credit for 7 days, but commonly the credit is extended for 30 days. Unfortunately many customers and clients consider there isn't a requirement to pay your invoice within the stipulated time period and will pay you perhaps after 60 days or even 90 days or more. So, the quicker they pay you; the smaller the number of days for accounts receivable and the better for you.

Accounts Payable Days – this is the opposite of accounts receivable days, as this shows the average number of days you take to pay your suppliers. In this case, within reason the higher the number, the better for your cashflow. However, it is important to pay your suppliers when they are expecting to be paid as this fosters goodwill with them. When you have a month with difficult cashflow it will make it easier to call them if you make it a regular practice to pay on time, then you can advise that you will be taking a little longer than usual to pay their invoices that month. Many will consider offering you better pricing which will improve your profit margin if you are a reliable payer.

Current Ratio – this measures the liquidity of your business. It is the comparison of your current assets to your current liabilities. In most cases your current assets will principally be the cash in your bank account, the amount of accounts receivable and your inventory at cost. Your current liabilities will principally be the amount of accounts payable, your bank overdraft if you have one and your tax and payroll liabilities. The bigger the current ratio the better as it indicates you have assets more than sufficient to meet your liabilities.

Quick Ratio – this is similar to the current ratio except it only uses cash and accounts receivable in the calculation. This is a better measure of whether you will be able to pay your liabilities in the short-term.

Inventory turnover– if your business has inventory it is important that you work out how to hold the optimum amount of stock at any point in time. The inventory turnover will indicate how many times a year you are replenishing your inventory. The higher the number, the better, as it indicates you are buying your stock when you need it and aren't holding stock for long periods of time without selling it. If you import goods it may not be possible to obtain the stock regularly as there is a long lead time from when you order to when the stock arrives at your business, in which case you will have a small inventory turnover.

One of the benefits of this KPI is knowing what your stock turnover is and then dissecting this figure down to each stock item or group of similar items to see whether you can order less frequently, not run out of stock and still sell the same number.

Gross Profit Margin – this is a percentage representing the net profit of the business divided by turnover (total sales revenue). If your business sells goods, the gross profit margin will be the difference between your selling price and the cost of goods divided by turnover expressed as a percentage. The higher the percentage the better as the more profit you will be making from each sale. If your business sells services, the cost of sales will be your employment costs and the gross profit margin will indicate how much profit you have made from selling the hours of your employees divided by turnover expressed as a percentage.

There are, of course, many others, and some which are simple, like the total revenue for the period, the net profit for the period which shows exactly how much profit you have made after taking into account all the expenses of running the business. Most of these figures are easily obtained from looking at the profit and loss statement or balance sheet discussed previously.

Specific KPI'S

Average spend per customer – this requires keeping a record of the number of customers in your point of sale system, and dividing the total revenue by the number of customers. Once you know what the average is, you can then concentrate on finding strategies to increase this figure. Think of McDonald's standard line of, "Would you like fries with that?" Once they are in your shop or restaurant, they are already buying from you, what other item can you suggest which would complement their purchase and increase the amount they spend?

Return on space – this is a fantastic KPI if you have a retail bricks and mortar store as it gives you an indication of how much money you are making per square meter or foot of space in your shop. When you have good reporting on your stock sales and are able to determine how much of each item you are selling, you can then break this down further to determine which product lines are really providing you with the best return on your rental cost. If, for example, you find that some lines take up a lot of space and you don't sell many of them, you might consider whether you need to be stocking those items and whether you might not be better off selling something else in that space that will give you a better return.

Gross Profit per Product Line – most businesses sell a number of different products or services. Some will cost more, some less. Some you can charge a higher margin on and others you can't. The benefit of knowing how much you are making on each product or service allows you to decide whether to keep offering those lower profit products or services. It may be that they are an integral part of what you do and they may be lead generation lines which get your customers or clients in the door and from which you can then sell your higher profit items. If that is the case, knowing which ones do make the least profit will allow you to focus on how you can perhaps reduce the cost of the item. Is there a cheaper supplier, can you do a better deal with your current supplier to reduce the cost, is there a more efficient way of doing this which would reduce the cost? Or you simply may have to accept that this is the way it is and concentrate on ensuring that the customers or clients do buy your higher profit items too.

Other non financial KPI'S

Some of the non financial KPI's can be a great indication of the good and the bad of your business. These require additional record keeping to determine, but are well worth the effort as the results may well surprise you. Some examples are:

Customer Satisfaction – this can be done by surveying your customers to determine their satisfaction with the business. This is very useful for a motor mechanic, or a tradesman, for example. It can be especially useful if you have a team of employees who are doing the work to keep track of how well they are liked by the customers. This can also be used to determine who is doing really well and who isn't which allows you to do more training with those who need it and reward those who are doing a good job.

Sales Conversions – this shows what percentage of leads or potential customers or clients actually turn into sales. This is a vital KPI for keeping track of your sales people and to support and train those who are not performing as well as those who are. It may allow you to find out exactly who is doing the best and then get them to mentor and coach the others as to how that person does it so everyone in the sales team gets the benefit of this knowledge and ability and the overall sales conversions will improve.

Website Traffic – with an increase in online business it is imperative to measure how well your website is performing. In essence, your website is like another sales person. You need to manage it, measure it and take appropriate action to improve it. Using Google Analytics, for example, will tell you a number of different figures for your website which allows you to track the effect of changes to ensure you improve the results each time.

Effective Hourly Rate – if your business sells time, this is a vital figure to measure. This takes the total income for the period, divides it by the number of hours of work your team has available to determine the effective hourly rate. As some of your team may be charged out at higher rates than others, and some, the administration staff, may not be charged out at all, the average hourly rate is a good indicator of how well you are recovering the costs of your staff and covering the overheads of the business. The higher the effective hourly rate is the better.

Using monthly management reports to focus on the key areas of the business

For the past few years, Heather and Harry have been running a very successful design agency. They had a bookkeeper who came into the office one day a week who looked after the bookkeeping using desktop accounting software. The bank reconciliations were done on a monthly basis after the paper bank statement was received from the bank and as a result the reports were always issued at least two weeks after the end of the month. During the course of the month, they had no idea how the business was tracking.

They came to me looking for an accountant to do more than simply prepare financial statements and tax returns as they wanted to have advice and input throughout the year. We discussed using a cloud accounting system and after seeing a demonstration of how it works, they decided it would be perfect for their requirements. They decided they would no longer need the services of the bookkeeper and would do the work required themselves.

The benefit of the bank data feeds and being able to invoice themselves when the job was completed, rather than waiting for the bookkeeper to come in to prepare the invoices was a much more efficient alternative for them. However, their main criteria was they wanted good reporting to show them how they were going and preferably in a visual format for ease of understanding. With the reporting options we have available with the cloud accounting system, we are able to produce a fourteen page report within a couple of days of the end of the month which had graphs and diagrams to show the figures in addition to the numbers. There were 40 Key Performance Indicators included in the report and both Heather and Harry were elated that they had reports which they were able to understand more easily.

In addition, they are now able to keep track on how the figures are going throughout the month by looking at the dashboard report within the cloud system. We recently reviewed the KPI's and discussed at length some issues which these figures highlighted, specifically that their income was sporadic, lurching from months with high income to months with very low income. Heather and Harry are now able to focus more closely on strategies to smooth out the cashflow and improve the workflow to get the jobs completed more quickly to get the income flowing.

Summary

1   Basic financial reports are the foundation for information for every business.

2   It is imperative to set goals for the Key Performance Indicators for your business and monitor your results.

3   Non financial Key Performance Indicators are crucial to truly understanding the core requirements of your business.

Chapter 11

Reviewing reports regularly

Dashboard report

The *dashboard report* is essential to look at on a daily basis, preferably at the beginning of the day. This gives you a snapshot of how the business is performing. Armed with this information, you will make better decisions during the course of the day to improve upon areas that need it throughout your working hours.

Accounts receivable report

The *accounts receivable* is a vital report to be reviewed. I suggest that you should look at this weekly, however, for some businesses you will need to look at it daily. The benefit of using cloud accounting systems means the information in the report is accurate daily if the basic bank reconciliations and invoicing are done regularly.

You need to look at this report daily if you have cashflow problems. If you have sufficient cashflow to pay the current week's expenses, then a review of the accounts receivable report on a weekly basis may be sufficient. While you are reviewing this report, you need to concentrate on customers or clients who are showing with amounts owing for the longest period of time. These will need to be followed up with a phone call to ask them to pay the account or to find out exactly when the account will be paid. For those customers or clients who owe money beyond your credit terms (whether they are seven days, 14 days or 30 days), either a reminder email or phone call will be necessary to find out why the account has not been paid. In some cases you may find that your customer or client is not happy with the goods or services or not happy with the amount of the invoice and you will need to deal with this first before they will pay.

What is vital is that you do follow up your outstanding customers or clients regularly. If they know that you will be chasing them up, they are more likely to pay your invoices on time in the future.

If you find that you have a customer or client who is not paying your invoices, you may have to make the decision to stop providing them with credit and not sell them anything more until their account is paid up to date. In the worst cases, you may need to employ the services of a debt collection agency or lawyers to seek recovery of the money owed to you.

Accounts payable report

The *accounts payable report* will show you how much you owe your suppliers. If your suppliers all provide you with 30 days credit, then in theory you only need to look at this report once a month to pay the bills. However, it is prudent to review this at a minimum of twice a month as you will have some suppliers who will require payment in less than 30 days.

For efficient processing of payments, a fortnightly or monthly review and processing of payments will simplify your accounting process and be more effective from both a time and cost perspective.

Cashflow forecast report

The *cashflow forecast report* is vital and must be reviewed regularly, if not daily then at least once a week. The good cloud accounting systems allow you to enter dates into the accounts receivable system to show when you expect your invoices to be paid. This information may come from phoning up and asking your customer or clients when they will pay and then updating your system accordingly. You can also enter into the accounts payable when you plan to make the payments to your suppliers. The benefit of doing this is the cashflow forecast will show you whether there will be sufficient money in your bank account to pay your suppliers when you plan to or not. It also helps to focus on getting more money in your bank account if you are short as you will know exactly how much you need to pay your bills.

Using the reporting for weekly meetings with management team

Marilyn owns a personal training gym, but she doesn't work in the business. Rather she is the overall manager and has spent her time in sales and marketing and undertaking the administration work. She has a management team in place to attend to the daily processes and manage the team who work in the business.

We established a cloud accounting system for the business after Marilyn complained of spending enormous amounts on a bookkeeper which seemed unnecessarily expensive for the size of the business at *the time. Marilyn has a corporate background and has a good overall knowledge of accounting and finances; however, she had no bookkeeping experience. In no time at all, she picked up the cloud system and was happily reconciling the bank account and undertaking the other bookkeeping functions.*

The best part of the system for Marilyn is the ability to print off reports at the end of the week to use in the weekly management meeting. The reports are used to set goals for the ensuing week, to make decisions on what marketing needs to be done, whether certain purchases for the business should be made and so on. In the beginning, the management team were amazed at how Marilyn was able to produce these reports in such a timely manner and so frequently. After a month of using these reports, they are now a fundamental part of how the business is operated.

Profit and loss statement

The *profit and loss statement* is best looked at on a monthly basis. The reason for this is expenses are paid on different days throughout the month so looking at this report throughout the month will give a distorted view of the trading results. For example, if you pay the rent for your business premises on the first day of the month, the expenses will be high compared to the rest of the month. Similarly, employee wages will be paid perhaps weekly or fortnightly and in some cases monthly. Depending upon when the paydays fall there will be times in the month which will have higher costs than for the month as a whole.

Even with looking at the profit and loss statement on a monthly basis, there will still be times when the figures will be skewed. For example, when you pay your business insurances in one payment for the twelve months, or when you have five weekly paydays, or three fortnightly paydays in a particular month.

Having said this, it is important you review the profit and loss statement at the end of each month after all the income and expenses have been entered into your accounting system and the bank accounts have been reconciled as this will show you whether you are actually making any money (profit) and if so, how much.

Management reports

Management reports take a number of different forms, from the standard basic reports of the profit and loss statement, balance sheet, accounts receivable and accounts payable reports, to more detailed reports which include key performance indicators (KPIs). The beauty of the better cloud accounting systems is you are able to obtain detailed management reports which provide all the figures you need, plus the KPIs and will show many of these figures in a graphical format. Like the dashboard, good management reports with graphs and charts are easy to understand and they provide visual aids reflecting what is happening in your business without wading through pages of numbers which can be difficult to understand.

Management reports are best prepared by your accountant so they can bring to your attention matters which require your urgent attention within the figures. These are a great starting point for conversations with your accountant on what changes you are considering and how they may impact the figures, and also what changes you may need to make to improve the financial performance of the business.

Reviewing management reports monthly is imperative if you want your business to flourish and grow. Even if you don't want to grow the business, it is important to review the management reports on a monthly basis to ensure you are maintaining the business at the level you want.

Too many times I have seen businesses get into financial difficulty because they failed to review their reports on a monthly basis and were unaware of how bad the figures really were until it was too late.

Management Reports Help Make
Business Decisions

Suzy runs a training business and also rents out the training rooms to other businesses to use for their training programs. Suzy keeps her records in two systems, one using spreadsheets and one through desktop accounting software. Unfortunately, neither system provides her with useful and reliable reports.

Suzy's old accountant didn't take any real interest in her business and so a couple of years passed with no reporting, not even the annual financial statements were prepared. Suzy approached me and begged for help to get her records up to date and prepare and lodge her tax returns and GST returns. Suzy really had no idea how the business was going although she knew business was tough and she expected she had made massive losses over the period.

I helped Suzy first by converting information from her past accounting systems onto a cloud accounting system to make it easier to bring the figures up to date. We then discovered she spent around $ 100,000 fitting out the business premises. This amount was not deductible for tax purposes and consequently, the business had in fact made a substantial profit in the first year upon which she owed around $30,000 *of income tax. The second year was a loss and no tax was payable for that year.*

Suzy is now reviewing her reports on a regular basis and knows exactly how much income she must make to break even. She is concentrating on bringing in more business and making sure that the training rooms are used five days a week with programs she is running or hired out to other businesses.

Tax reports

One of the biggest mistakes you can make is to spend the tax man's money you have collected and are due to pay him in the future. Whether this is the GST, VAT, State Taxes, Federal Taxes, Sales Tax, Tax deducted from employees' wages, it doesn't matter. As far as the tax man is concerned it is his money, not yours. You simply shouldn't be spending it; rather you should be putting it aside so you can pay the tax man when he is due to be paid.

I recommend that you check the amount of tax you owe the tax man on a weekly basis and transfer that money into a separate bank account which is only used to pay the tax man when you have to. In this way, the money you have in your bank account is the money you have earned from your business and is the amount you have left over to pay your suppliers, employees and yourself. No more, no less.

At the end of the month, you should check the total due to the tax man and compare that to the money in the separate bank account. If you have extra in the separate bank account, you then have the option to transfer that back in the business bank account as it is your money. However, if you transfer the correct amount each week, when you check at the end of the month, the money in the separate bank account should be the correct amount.

You might even consider setting up a second separate bank account and transfering money into that as a savings account for yourself. There is nothing better than knowing you have some money saved to give you peace of mind that you have sufficient money to pay the bills in the business. Too many people have sleepless nights worrying about how they will be able to pay the rent, the wages, and the suppliers. You don't have to be one of them.

Summary

1   Nothing replaces the value of reviewing the accounting reports of your business on a regular basis.

2   The old saying, "What you measure, you can manage," is so true, but without reviewing the reports, there is no point measuring.

3   A meeting or conversation with your accountant to review the reports will provide further insight into your business and suggestions on areas you need to focus on to improve.

Chapter 12

How to choose a good accountant to partner with

Choosing the right accountant to partner with in your business is vital. However, the decision on who to choose can be difficult. At the end of the day you need to feel comfortable talking to the person and you need to feel they are prepared to listen to you and provide advice to help you along the way.

A good accountant will truly help with your business and provide invaluable advice on what to do and what not to do. They will share their experiences and those of their clients who had similar experiences; they will refer you to experts when they don't have the expertise and will generally be a sounding board for new ideas and plans for the business.

An experienced business accountant will also assist with strategies to maximise the value of the business when you plan to sell, they will assist with the transfer of the business to the next generation if you want to keep the business in the family and a host of other business related queries and suggestions.

Questions to ask

So, the big question is... how do you know if an accountant is the right accountant for you?

You will need to ask a series of questions when you first meet with an accountant and you may need to meet with a few before you make a decision. Most accountants will offer a complimentary first meeting for about an hour. During this meeting you need to find out as much as you can about the accountant, and similarly, the accountant will be finding out as much as possible about you to decide whether they want to work with you. It is a bit like a two-way interview, or a first date, where you will both be assessing if you are compatible.

Bear in mind there are no right or wrong answers, however, some of the basic questions to ask are:

How long have they been in business?

This will establish how much experience they bring to the table. An accountant with years of experience will have better insight and will be able to share past business experiences with you, where appropriate.

An accountant who has recently branched out on their own may have the knowledge and know how to help your business; however, they may not be able to allocate as much time to you as a client. They will probably still be learning the ropes of starting a new business and their focus may shift to this instead of providing you the service you deserve.

How many staff and what qualifications?

This will give you an idea of whether you will get the personal attention of the accountant you are meeting with or whether you will be dealing with the employees or other people in the business. The bigger the accounting firm, the more likely it is you won't get much of the principal accountant's time unless you are a large client for them. It is also important to know whether the staff has qualifications or not. With the smaller firms, if there are qualified staff in addition to the accountant you are dealing with, it means you will still be able to get answers to your technical questions even if the principal accountant is not available.

Unless you are dealing with a one man office, the staff will be the ones who will be carrying out a majority of the number crunching, preparing the financial statements and tax returns and attending to compliance matters. This leaves the principal with more time for meeting with you to provide advice and being available to answer your questions as they arise.

What accounting systems do they support for their clients?

This is a vital question. You need to make sure the accounting firm you will be dealing with uses the system you will be using. This has always been the case, although it is even more imperative with cloud accounting systems as your accountant will need to have access to the cloud accounting system to review and correct the entries when necessary. They will also need access to the system to produce their management reports. Ideally, you want your accounting firm to set up the cloud accounting system for you, to provide you with training and phone/email support when you have questions. The better cloud accounting systems have excellent help sections which will answer your questions on the how to, but what they don't answer are the specific questions which relate to your industry or your particular business in how you set up the system to give you the best possible reporting.

If your accountant does not use and support the accounting system you intend to use, you should expect to pay more for them to prepare the financial statements and tax returns and you will have to provide them with a lot more information so they can work for you. This can be frustrating and time consuming, as well as more costly.

Do they have names of three clients in either similar industries or similar stages in the business cycle to phone for references?

Some people think they need to use an accountant with many clients in the same industry as them in order to get the best advice. There are some advantages to this; however, what is often lost when an accounting firm specialises in one industry is the application of ideas from other industries. From an accounting perspective, one business is principally the same as another. They all sell something, pay expenses and hopefully make a profit. They all have money in the bank, some have accounts receivable and inventory, all have accounts payable and tax liabilities. The difference lies in the detail of the actual business and a good accountant will be able to use experiences from one industry and apply that knowledge to the next business seamlessly thus providing a different perspective.

What is important though is to speak to some of the clients of the accounting firm to find out about their experience with their accountant, how often they see them, how accessible they are, how quickly they get the work done, what other services they use, how useful has the business advice been and so on.

The most relevant references will be the ones from businesses who are at the same stage as you, whether that is in start up, early commercial phase (a couple of years after start up when the business is profitable), mature business or proposing to sell. Some accountants specialise in start-ups and micro businesses and don't have any experience with mature businesses. Others will cover the full spectrum.

Do they survey their clients for feedback to improve?

Many accounting firms operate their businesses based on what the tax man requires them to do and they don't pay any attention to whether they are providing the services their clients really want. The better firms survey their clients and get feedback on ways to improve. When you are seeking an accounting firm you want to make sure your accountant is always looking for ways to improve their business as they will be the best to help you improve yours.

What is the client retention rate?

The answer to this question may be quite interesting. Although, I will hazard a guess that most accountants won't know what the correct answer is to this question and will provide you with a glib response that their clients have been with them for x number of years. If the accountant is losing clients regularly they are not going to want to answer this question as it would indicate they are not providing good service to their clients.

What you are seeking to find out here is whether the accountant has clients who have been loyal for many years, whether they have a lot of new clients and if possible whether they have been losing clients.

Who is their ideal client?

This question will give you an idea of whether you are the right fit for the accountant. It will also give you some idea of where you will come in the pecking order from the perspective of the accountant. If you fit their profile of the ideal client, you should expect you will receive excellent service and will be well looked after. If your business is not quite their ideal client, but you tick the majority of the boxes, then you will also be a good fit. However, if you only tick a few of the boxes, then you may not be well served by that accountant and would be better to continue looking for an alternative.

Many accountants try to be all things to all clients. This is not a good business model for any business, and as such, you may or may not have the right accountant if he or she is unable to articulate their ideal client.

What are their service standards?

You need to find out what service standards the accounting firm operates with. These are matters like how quickly will they respond to phone calls and emails, what time frame will they get the annual financial statements and tax returns completed in, what are their payment terms, will they accept monthly payments, what systems do they have in place to ensure you meet all your tax deadlines.

What to look out for
Overall state of the office

I find it fascinating when I go to business premises to see how tidy it is or not. The state of the business owner's office is usually a good indication of whether the business is being run well and is organised and how good the accounting records are likely to be.

The same applies to accountants. If the accountant has papers in a mess, and there are piles of paper all around the office, and it is generally messy, chances are the accountant may not be providing timely service to their clients.

If the accountant's office is neat and tidy, this shows they are organised and efficient and more likely to provide timely service and good advice.

How fancy is the office?

This will provide you with an indication of the level of fees you may be paying and whether you are paying for the advice and services or whether you are paying for your accounting firm to have fancy offices for themselves.

Certainly, you want to be partnering with an accounting firm which is successful. After all, if your accountant is successful, then they will be in a far better position to provide good advice to you for your business than if they are not successful. There are accounting firms who do have large reception areas, are located in the best building, paying the highest rent, have expensive furniture and provide good advice; however, their fee level will be significantly higher than other firms who don't have all the luxuries. At the end of the day, you shouldn't mind paying high fees as long as you are getting good value for money. I, too, fail to see why my hard earned money should be spent on providing unnecessary fancy offices to people I do business with if I am not getting value.

Perception of value for service

Karen came for an initial complimentary meeting to discuss her accounting and taxation requirements. Karen was cost conscious and wanted to ensure she was getting value for the fees being paid. Her big concern was that although she understood an accountant is in business to make money, just like she is, she wanted to make sure the fees she would be paying weren't going to be funding fancy offices forthe accountant or an excessive lifestyle.

As part of the interview process, she asked questions about the number of staff employed by the firm, who would actually be doing the work, who would be her point of contact when she had questions, and wanted to see the whole office to determine whether the accounting firm was being run well with good resources and no excesses.

I think we all want the people we do business with to be successful, but we don't want to see them living a highly exorbitant lifestyle especially when they are giving financial advice. We like to do business with people like ourselves, people who share our values and ethics. Those who are honest, ethical and have high morals want to have their business partners with those same standards. Those who want to cheat and lie, and do dodgy deals want to have business partners who will turn a blind eye to those actions or who actively encourage them. At the end of the day, we all attract people who are like us and when interviewing an accountant you need to be able to determine whether they are like you or not.

Does the accountant listen to what you say?

As is often quoted, you have one mouth and two ears, you should use them proportionately. Your accountant should also abide by this, they need to listen to what you say and truly understand your issues and try to answer your questions. There is no point in having an accountant who tells you what to do without asking you lots of questions to fully understand what your issues are before providing the advice.

After your initial meeting with the accountant, consider how much talking you did, and how much talking the accountant did. Also, did the accountant actually hear what you said and respond to it, or did you just get the standard wording that did not reflect any comprehension of what you said.

Do you feel any rapport?

This is vital. You need to feel there is some rapport between you and your accountant. Once you are in the relationship and working with your accountant, you have to feel you can tell them anything and everything. Your accountant needs to know exactly what is going on in your business, and in many cases issues in your personal life too as they will impact the business. You need to feel you will be comfortable having these conversations with your accountant. If you have good rapport, your accountant will always be on your side; they will empathise with you, understand what you are dealing with and be able to provide specific advice to help you.

"I Think I love My Accountant"

After many years of using a bookkeeper for their pharmacy business, Alan and Anne decided to find a new accountant. They felt their bookkeeper was always working in the best interests of the tax man. After looking around, they came to me and felt a good rapport.

After a few months working with my firm, they mentioned how happy they were that after years in the wilderness, they now felt their accountant was on their side and working in their best interests, whilst still complying with the law.

Does the accountant understand the issues you have?

This comes back to the question of how much experience the accountant has. The more experience, the more likely they are to understand the issues you have. However, you will only know this if you raise a particular issue at the initial meeting to see whether they will acknowledge and comprehend the types of issues you are likely to be dealing with.

You may be having issues with finding the right staff, managing staff, cashflow problems, pricing issues, lack of consistent quality, poor accounting records and a myriad of other issues, all of which a good business accountant will have come across before and be able to provide advice to help you work through them.

Query about the acquisition of major equipment

Richard is in the food manufacturing business with a factory which is spic and span. Interestingly, his accounting records and paperwork are similarly spic and span. He is an accountant's dream as his records are kept meticulously. Like any successful businessman, Richard keeps up to date with the changes in his industry and the new equipment which is available overseas. He wanted to buy a machine to perform a particular function for some time as it would increase the capacity of the business and reduce the reliance on manual labour for this particular function.

He came to me to discuss a number of factors relating to the proposal to acquire the machinery. His biggest issues in his mind to start with were could he afford it and where could he put it logistically in his business premises. We talked about the existing design of the factory floor and what could be moved around to determine where the machine would fit in best. We also talked about the possibility of relocating the entire factory so that he could fit in this machine; however, that would have been a very costly solution. The decision was made to re-arrange two other machines so there would be sufficient space for the new machine.

Then we discussed the financing and taxation aspects of the acquisition. This involved a review of the various alternative types of finance and the tax effects of each. In addition, as the machine was being acquired from overseas, we also had to factor in the possibility of a fluctuating exchange rate given there would be some months from the date of the order to the date of delivery, installation and subsequent payment. We discussed ways to reduce the currency fluctuation risk and the decision to go ahead and buy the machine was made.

Two years later, and that decision has been one of the best decisions for the business. The increased capacity allowed him to take on some one-off manufacturing requests which he wouldn't have been able to do previously. The quality control and speed of processing has reduced his requirement for casual labour and overtime from his staff. In addition, changes in consumer demand have meant that the machine is used more than he had envisaged when he decided to buy it and again this has improved his profits.

Has your potential new accountant checked for any information about you or your business before your first appointment?

When you made the appointment to meet with an accountant, they should have asked some basic questions about what you are doing and your requirements. If they have done this properly they would have found out the details of your website and what industry you are in.

Before the meeting, a good accountant will have looked at your website, Googled you, and checked out your social media presence and if you are in an industry which is unknown to them, they would have completed some research on the industry. You will be able to work out very quickly whether the accountant has done this or not. If they have, it shows they are interested in finding out more about you and whether you are an ideal client for them.

If they haven't done any research before the meeting, this may indicate a lack of interest in the business and they may only provide compliance services not business advice and support.

However, if you are a start-up without a website, depending upon whether you have advised the sort of business you are planning to start, it may be difficult for the accountant to do any research work before the meeting. This doesn't mean they are not interested in what you are doing, it just means you will need to determine their level of interest and enthusiasm for your business from the meeting itself.

Will they customise their service, or is it a one size fits all?

Most accountants will discuss your requirements at the initial meeting and determine what services you require. Traditionally, accountants have charged their clients based on the time spent on doing the job. However, this system is archaic and allows for accounting firms to be highly inefficient with you, the client, footing the bill for their staff to learn on the job. Better accounting firms now will provide fixed fee quotes for the work. This means that you know what the costs will be before the work is started and you can negotiate the fees at that time. Then it is up to the accountant to make sure they do the job as efficiently as possible to make a profit.

A number of accounting firms, now offer bundled services which include annual financial statements, tax returns, management reporting, regular meetings and so on. These services are ideal because for one fee you get everything you need to ensure you keep track of the business and are held accountable for your goals on a regular basis.

Summary

1   A good accountant will provide advice and encouragement.

2   The right accountant will become your confidante and an integral part of your business and decision making.

3   You should feel comfortable approaching your accountant to ask any question relating to the business, and to discuss personal issues which may have an impact on your financial position.

Chapter 13

The future of computing

There are so many exciting innovations looming on the horizon now. The benefits which can be gained by businesses embracing these changes are potentially massive and for those who continually are seeking ways to improve the efficiencies of their business, there is no better time than now to focus on this.

Automatic integration of invoices into purchases in customer or client cloud accounting records

As more and more integration of information is available within your business, so too will be the opportunity to integrate your business' information with your customers or clients and your suppliers. For example, Xero has launched the integration of invoicing between businesses. If you issue an invoice to your customer or client who also uses Xero and has given you permission to do so, your invoice will automatically appear in their Xero system as an amount owing to your business. Cool, eh. Now isn't this a wonderful way to ensure that your customers or clients can't say that they didn't receive the invoice?

No more burning data onto a CD or USB stick

With the improvements in security of using the cloud for data storage and more people embracing this as an alternative to using your own hard drive or back-up storage, the need to use a CD or USB stick will be removed. In years to come these will be obsolete. Consider how not that long ago, we used to have to back-up everything onto a back-up tape system or onto a CD. Not many businesses are still using the CD as a backup storage solution today. External hard drives and USB sticks are frequently used today, but I doubt that they will be as frequently used in a year or two.

Use of Dropbox, iCloud and Google+ and other document sharing platforms

The use of systems like Dropbox, iCloud and Google+ will see more and more businesses using these storage solutions for all their business records and the need for PCs with internal hard drives will be eliminated. iPad's and tablets will take over from the PCs as the device of choice. The collaboration with other users available through these document sharing platforms is impressive. If your business functions around the world, these systems will allow access to everyone you give access to, whether your, your virtual team overseas, your graphic designer or copywriter locally or overseas, your suppliers or customers locally or overseas. You just pick and choose who has access to which documents and instantly those people have access. No more emailing documents or even mailing them.

Keyboard and mouse to be obsolete with more touchscreen capabilities

The keyboard and mouse have been with us for a long time, but their life expectancy has been significantly shortened. Touchscreen capability which was first introduced by Apple is now prevalent on other SmartPhones, the Window Surface tablet and a host of others. Consider the large computer table system which was used on the recent Hawaii Five-O TV series. The team was showcasing the future of our computer systems with easy access to a myriad of different systems with the touch of a finger or the swiping of a hand.

Desktop computers will be obsolete – everyone will be using mobile devices – iPads, Tablets or SmartPhones in the future

We are living in a technology age of rapid change. Business types have also been changing in recent years with the growth of businesses which are solely based on the internet, the demise of the traditional retail sector, and the growth of innovative different businesses which didn't exist five or 10 years ago. Businesses are more mobile, with people working from home more, or from coffee shops and not in a traditional office environment. Many more businesses do not have a traditional office or business premises. The future will be more usage of mobile devices and considerably less reliance on desktop computers.

Voice recognition and instructions

The next logical step will be the use of voice recognition systems to perform tasks. Voice recognition has been available for many years; however, there have been challenges with it and to date it has not received popular support. But as we move away from the keyboard and mouse, I believe that voice recognition will be more prevalent and available for more applications.

Summary

1   There are many more innovations still to come.

2   Beware investing in current hardware and consider what the future might hold.

3   Many of the systems you currently use will be obsolete in the near future.

Chapter 14

Where to from here?

There are a few fundamental decisions you need to make.

Firstly, do you want to embrace new technology and improve the efficiencies of your business?

If you do, then secondly, you need to decide which cloud accounting system will be the best for your business.

Thirdly, you may need to consider finding a new accountant who will proactively work with you to grow and improve your business.

Consider the following examples:

Getting advice before starting a new business

Mary and David were starting up a new business providing professional consulting services. The first step they took was to find an accountant and following a referral from a friend, they landed at my door full of enthusiasm, eager to learn. We discussed in detail what their plans were for the business along with their long-term goals.

We then recommended a specific business structure allowing flexibility where required and providing asset protection and the opportunity to minimise tax along the way. As part of the process we then discussed the need for keeping accounting records, reviewed the alternatives available and recommended a cloud accounting system as it is easy to use and doesn't require a massive time commitment to maintain.

Not getting proper advice to start with

Matthew is a tradesman who was working principally as a sub-contractor when he and his wife came to see me. They were using a bookkeeper to lodge their quarterly Business Activity Statements (BAS) and an accountant who they were concerned wasn't claiming all the deductions they were entitled to. Sandra was spending four or five days at the end of each quarter putting all the information into a spreadsheet to send to the bookkeeper.

I reviewed their financial reports and asked a number of questions and determined they hadn't received advice when they set up the business and were inadvertently breaching half a dozen different laws. We reviewed each, one by one, and determined what action needed to be taken to rectify the issues. Some we needed to go back and lodge amended returns, some we registered at that time. They had both been completely unaware of the issues and had believed they were doing the right thing.

It is imperative when you start out in business, to seek the services of an experienced business accountant who will ensure you do have all the right registrations, licences, insurances, and that tax requirements are met.

We set up the business on a cloud accounting system, trained Sandra on how to use the system. She now says that she spends only an hour or two at the end of the quarter preparing the figures for the quarterly BAS. She regularly reconciles the bank account and actually enjoys doing the bookwork.

Using spreadsheets and losing sleep

Tracy and her husband, Brian, have been running their catering business for over 10 years. During this time it has grown from one business, to a business with three distinct components. Like many wives, Tracy is in charge of the bookkeeping and accounting for the business in addition to helping in the business too. With the support of her accountant and no advice to the contrary for years Tracy was maintaining a spreadsheet to keep track of the finances. The spreadsheet was one sheet for payments from the bank account, one for receipts into the bank account and another for cash expenses. She was painstakingly recording every payment, receipt and the details of the GST components.

In the early years, this system worked quite well. There wasn't a massive volume of transactions, and she was able to reconcile the figures against her bank statement on a regular basis. However, in recent years, the business has grown to include not only catering services, but now a café too. She works even more hours in the business in addition to looking after the bookkeeping and paperwork and as a result, the spreadsheet system has become a major chore and very time consuming.

For many months, Tracy recorded the transactions, but she didn't have the time to reconcile each entry against her bank statements to make sure the information was complete and accurate. As a result, she failed to lodge her BAS and pay the tax man for the money she owed. As a good, moral and ethical citisen, this didn't sit well with her and she was losing sleep worrying about it.

Tracy came to me to seek advice about a better option of keeping her accounting records. Her old accountant was not forthcoming with any advice in this area and left her to do what she wanted without any suggestions for improvements. We discussed her requirements, and decided she would gain massive benefits from using a cloud accounting system with the data feeds from the bank accounts saving on the data entry requirements and allowing for the bank account to be reconciled much quicker and easier. We set up the system for her and imported in the transactions from the beginning of the current financial year to make sure the full years' transactions were in the one system.

She has undertaken some training, both one on one and in a group and is now happily using the system and enjoying the process. It is no longer the burden it once was and she and her husband are now able to see how their business is running with the push of a button by reviewing the reports within the system.

One of the major downsides of using spreadsheets for accounting purposes is you don't get any reports and mostly the figures will not provide you with much insight as to how well the business is doing.

We are now looking at installing a point of sale system to integrate with the cloud accounting system and will also be looking at integrating her shopping cart from one of her websites where she does a significant quantity of sales.

The moral of the story

Be brave, take a risk and move onto a cloud accounting system. After you have made the switch you will never look back and wonder why you fussed about whether to make the change.

Find an accountant to work with to grow your business and reduce the stress and time consuming components of the bookkeeping. You will have better reports to make better business decisions and you will have time to concentrate on ensuring your business flourishes in the coming years. Cloud accounting allows you to feel in control of your business and provides you with meaningful information on a regular basis.

ABOUT THE AUTHOR

Amanda Fisher is a Fellow of the Institute of Chartered Accountants in Australia and has over 30 years experience working with successful small to medium businesses. She has been a partner in two accounting practices and run two of her own accounting practices. In addition she has worked as a financial controller and company accountant and understands the time and effort involved in maintaining accurate accounting records for businesses.

Amanda has been an early adopter of new accounting technology throughout her career and is passionate about the impact cloud based accounting systems can have on business owners and their lives. These systems are revolutionising the way business owners can operate their businesses, helping to minimise bookkeeping time and have up to date, accurate financial information immediately available at all times.

Amanda works with business owners who are keen to improve their business, improve cashflow, increase their turnover and have time for their families and personal interests. Her favourite businesses are catering contractors, food manufacturers, medical professionals, pharmacies, graphic designers, internet based businesses and building trades.

Amanda would love to hear your feedback on the book, email her at: *amanda@connectedaccountants.com.au*

NEXT STEPS

Bonuses: Check out the bonuses offered throughout the book.

Communities: Join the Connected Accountants community at

> *www.facebook.com/ConnectedBusinessOwners*
> *www.LinkedIn.com/ConnectedBusinessOwners*

Other Resources: Check out other accounting related resources at

> *www.connectedaccountants.com.au*

Consultation: For a consultation, send an email to

> *amanda@connectedaccountants.com.au*

CONNECTED ACCOUNTANTS